Looking Back and Looking Forward…

Petersen Ranch | Fitzgerald | Dakota Vervain

Published by
Images for Conservation Fund (ICF)
2112 W. University Drive, #801
Edinburg, Texas 78539
Phone: 956-381-1264
Fax: 956-381-8422
Email: icfprotour@aol.com
www.imagesforconservation.org

Editor: Pat Rangel
Lead Writer: Diane Solether Smith
Book Designer: Judy Robertson Designs
Printer: Cockrell Printing, Ken Gaskins
Fort Worth, Texas

ISBN 1-4276-0703-6
First Printing, 2006
Printed in the U.S.A.

I remember the days when folks used to walk up to the house of the farmer or the rancher in Texas and ask if they could go onto the property to hunt, or fish…or whatever. After a little chit-chat to get acquainted, most likely the farmer or the rancher would say, "Sure, just leave the gates like you find them." In those days we didn't manage wildlife populations, or wildlife habitat; we just had whatever Mother Nature provided, or you might say that wildlife got whatever was left over. Those days are gone forever. In a way it is a shame; in a way it is a blessing.

Today the landowners who manage their habitat for more numerous and more diversified wildlife not only have great personal satisfaction in seeing the results of their efforts, but may also receive significant revenue from hunters, fishermen, wildlife photographers and wildlife watchers. The better the habitat and the more diversified the wildlife, the more they can charge and the more customers they will have.

Sometimes you hear folks complain about "having to pay" to enjoy the outdoors and the wildlife of our state and our nation. Not me; I don't "buy" that. Nothing is free. If we're going to have good birding, good properties to photograph wildlife…or to hunt, or to fish in the world today, somebody is going to pay and that "somebody" is you and I. If the private landowner goes to the expense and hard work to provide good birding, more birders are going to pay to get access to that area and enjoy the outdoors. If the government provides access to public land and good habitat for birding or outdoor recreation, someone must continue to pay for it, and, again, that someone is you and I.

We didn't do much to provide for wildlife back when I was a kid on the farm, and frankly, our habitat and our wildlife wasn't all that good either. It was "free"…but that was about all it was worth. Landowners today who provide great habitat, overnight lodging, meals, photo blinds, feeding stations, and four-wheeler access around the ranch are pretty much able to name their price, and they have to turn folks away to maintain a high quality experience for their birders, or hunters, or folks who just want to enjoy the outdoors. If you look at it closely, the data clearly indicates that the private landowner can provide quality outdoor experiences and quality habitat for less expense than the government. Times have changed, and our approach to the outdoors has changed. We know it is not free; we know that good habitat and good wildlife is not an accident in today's world. It doesn't just happen!

Get outdoors. Enjoy!

Bob Cook
Executive Director
Texas Parks & Wildlife Department

IMAGES FOR CONSERVATION | BOOK ONE
Texas Hill Country Edition

Keeler | Scarlet
Leatherflower

Species Identification: Wildlife Diversity Program Staff, Texas Parks & Wildlife Department
Contributors: Ernie Altgelt, Liz Carpenter, Bob Cook, Bob Hixon, Sherwood Inkley, Barbara Lipscomb, John F. Martin, Sam Mason, Shelly Parks, Bob Petersen
Photo credit for first page: Estrella Ranch | Nussbaumer | Lindheimer Prickly Pear

About Images for Conservation Fund...

Estrella Ranch | Nussbaumer
Juniper Hairstreak on Eve's Necklace

The images in this book represent the work of 17 of the world's finest nature photographers, taken over the course of 30 intense, sweaty, and difficult 18-hour days. The teams, 17 photographers and 17 landowners, were randomly paired to document the wildlife and landscapes of the Texas Hill Country and to compete in the world's richest photographic tournament. The inaugural ICF Pro-Tour of Nature Photography awarded $160,000 in cash, shared equally by the photographer and landowner of each winning team. The first grand prize of $64,000 was unprecedented.

The Mission of Images for Conservation Fund (ICF) is conservation of wildlife habitat using the power of nature photography while integrating art, education, economic development and natural history. Conservation is accomplished through the creation of wealth and the Pro-Tour is the primary tool for developing the Nature Photo Tourism Industry.

The concept evolved as a natural extension of my dream of saving wild lands through the creation of economic incentives for habitat protection. Ten years of experience with the Valley Land Fund (VLF) Wildlife Photo Contests in South Texas plus 30 years in wildlife conservation and business convinced me that if we were to truly save ecosystems it would have to come through economics.

The VLF experience showed that settings installed for the competitions–photo blinds, feeders and ponds–attracted photographers long after the contest, and they were willing to pay significant day fees. Landowners had a new income source potentially greater than anything else they had ever attempted.

In 2003, Sam Mason became the ICF's Executive Director and only paid staff person. While Sam wrote the by-laws, filed IRS forms and developed ICF's infrastructure, I recruited board members, partners, sponsors and participants for the inaugural 2006 Pro-Tour. My most important recruit was Bob Petersen, who dedicated two years of his life to the operations of the inaugural tournament.

The Texas Hill Country was selected because of its natural beauty and biodiversity. The region is susceptible to drought, fires and floods, making ranching income unreliable. The ever-increasing pressure to subdivide and develop is disrupting and in some cases destroying the complex ecosystems and placing ranchers in a position of fighting nature rather than fully utilizing nature as a source of income.

The purpose of the ICF Pro-Tour is to educate landowners and photographers about the value of private lands photography, to stimulate the demand for private lands as a destination for nature photographers and to encourage the preservation of natural habitat. For the first time in history, ranchers will be able to create income from nature's diversity.

John F. Martin, 2006
Founder, Images for Conservation Fund

Dedication to Lady Bird Johnson...

Welcome to the *Images for Conservation | Book One | Texas Hill Country Edition*, where you can feast your eyes on the poetry of this planet—wildflowers and wildlife that have been preserved by inspired Texas landowners and captured for all by camera.

Poetry? Yes, because photographs, like words, feed the soul.

The Images for Conservation Fund, which produces the Pro-Tour of Nature Photography, dedicates the inaugural book to Lady Bird Johnson, who inspired a nation and beyond, to protect the beauty of its native lands.

She began as a child seeking out the first violets of spring around the old cypress trees on Caddo Lake in her native East Texas. Her marriage led her to the Hill Country and its spring-fed streams and sudden spreads of bluebonnets, primroses, Indian Paintbrush, gaillardia, and picturesque plumes of native grasses.

Always when life led her to Washington, she reflects, "I cast a backward glance to the wide sweeping hills, the golden sunshine, the grey-green landscape of the Hill Country that I've come to love."

The award-winning photographs in this book are testimony to Lady Bird Johnson's appreciative eye and elegant words about the natural spots of our planet.

Liz Carpenter

Liz Carpenter

A native Texan, *Liz Carpenter* began her career as a political journalist covering the Franklin D. Roosevelt White House for the *Austin American-Statesman*.

During the LBJ administration, Liz served as press secretary and chief of staff for Lady Bird Johnson, with whom she has shared a deep and enduring friendship.

Lady Bird Johnson | photo courtesy of the Lady Bird Johnson Wildflower Center

About Estrella Ranch...

Nussbaumer | Claret Cup Cactus

Ruggedly beautiful Estrella Ranch is located over the Edwards Aquifer Recharge Zone, along the southern edge of the Edwards Plateau between Concan and Utopia in Uvalde County, Texas. Craggy hills drop as much as 500 feet into scenic valleys that remain relatively unaltered by human intrusion. Crystal clear water burbles from limestone canyon walls, cutting a cave-like pool into the 120 million-year-old Glen Rose strata. Tiny salamanders swim near primeval ferns and dinosaur tracks cut into the rock.

Raised in Germany for part of his childhood, petroleum geologist Robert L. Hixon fell in love with dramatic landscape. In the mid 1990's, a camping expedition introduced the Hixon family to Hamman Scout Ranch near Tarpley, sparking a three-year search for the roughest, rockiest, highest terrain they could find in the Texas Hill Country—the 790-acre Estrella Ranch. The contrasting topography offers excellent cover for wildlife with "multi-dimensional" ecosystems—springs, bottomland, high ridges, creeks, caves and meadows. Seeps and springs feed both the Blanco and Little Blanco Creeks. Two rocky ridges converge at Cougar Point, a dramatic overlook above Blanco Creek, offering breathtaking and unobstructed views.

Preservation and improvement of wildlife and plant habitats are primary goals for Estrella Ranch, which operates under a wildlife tax treatment. Carefully planned Ashe Juniper and brush clearing prepared sections of the property for seeding with native grass and forbs/wildflowers. Hixon has planted more than 400 native trees and shrubs along the Blanco Creek and its tributaries to improve the riparian buffer zone, protecting the fragile land from further erosion, improving water purity and offering protective cover for wildlife. Several fenced "exclosures" protect newly planted native species from the browsing deer and other wildlife.

Hixon has installed bird and bat houses for nesting and is introducing alternative water sources for wildlife throughout the ranch—liner tanks, steel tanks and "water guzzlers" (a tin roof and gutter with pipes and tanks set up to collect rainwater). Biologists and scientists from U.S. Fish and Wildlife, The Nature Conservancy, the

Audubon Society and Environmental Defense have documented the plant and wildlife species found on the ranch, including Hutton's Vireo, Painted Buntings and endangered Golden-cheeked Warblers and Black-capped Vireos.

The ranch has an amazing variety of plant life including Live Oak, Spanish Oak, Lacey Oak, Cedar Elm, Hackberry, Escarpment Cherry, Buckeye and Sycamore. Recent exploration has revealed a magnificent Texas Madrone tree hidden in an oak grove. The double-trunk tree, more than 50 feet high and with a crown over 50 feet in diameter, is one of the largest specimens known in the state. The Hixon family is still exploring the many ravines and ridgetops for new discoveries.

Bob and Cassie Hixon and their four children share their enthusiasm for the land with family and friends. Eagle Scout Matt and his dad regularly hosted scouting activities at the ranch; daughters Beth, Amy and Sarah have been inspired to studies in anthropology and zoology. Bob has sought to impress upon the children that many people might see a jungle or thicket on much of the ranch, but that "animals see the same thing and see places to live." Concerned that many areas of the beautiful Hill Country are being cleared, the family strives to support and protect the wildlife and the untamed beauty of the property. The Hixons' ultimate goal is to form a conservation easement for Estrella Ranch in order to prevent future development and to preserve the natural treasures they have come to love so much.

Photo courtesy of Bob Hixon

Estrella Ranch
Robert L. Hixon
Phone: (713) 495-6551
newriverex@aol.com

Photo courtesy of Bob Hixon

Rolf Nussbaumer

In his native Switzerland, Rolf spent his early adult years making furniture, teaching others the joys of birding and, as a hobbyist, shooting pictures. It wasn't long however before his hobby, coupled with his love of the outdoors, became an obsession—and then, his profession.

After marriage and a move to Texas, Rolf made the commitment to devote his energies full-time to wildlife photography. The decision proved to be a good one. Today, Rolf's award-winning work has been published in the United States, Europe and Asia. As a testament to his formidable skills, the self-taught naturalist won First Prize twice in the 2002 and 2004 Valley Land Fund's Wildlife Photo Contests. Rolf followed those victories with another first in the prestigious 2005 Coastal Bend Wildlife Photo Contest. Both of these events were held in his adored adopted state of Texas.

Rolf's personal mission is to help others experience nature through photography. He believes wildlife photography's main emphasis is "to show people things in their environment they usually wouldn't see." His cleverly executed shots of all things great and small, in their natural habitats and totally unaware of his presence, bring this mostly unknown world of the wild to an appreciative audience around the world.

New Braunfels, Texas
www.rolfnussbaumer.com

Nussbaumer | Rio Grande Leopard Frog

9

Nussbaumer | Nerve-Ray

Nussbaumer | Cecropia Moth

Nussbaumer | Praying Mantis

Nussbaumer | Virginia Opossum

Nussbaumer | Western Slimy Salamander

Nussbaumer | Bold Jumper

Nussbaumer | Northern Raccoon

Nussbaumer | Lindheimer Prickly Pear Cactus

Nussbaumer | Northern Mockingbird

Nussbaumer | Barking Frog

Nussbaumer | (L) Female Black-chinned Hummingbird and (R) Male Ruby-throated Hummingbird with a Prickly Pear Cactus

Nussbaumer | Eastern Fox Squirrel

Nussbaumer | Cliff Chirping Frog

Nussbaumer | Vervain

Nussbaumer | Striped Skunk

Nussbaumer | Cecropia Moth

About Knibbe Ranch...

Franz | Mexican Hat

Founded in 1852, the 1,000-acre Knibbe Ranch is one of the few remaining Century Heritage Ranches in Texas. Fifth generation owner Charles J. "Chuck" Knibbe and his wife Sharon, with their children Shannon and Chad, manage the property located along the Guadalupe River in Spring Branch, Comal County, Texas. Lone Star flags flank a cedar post entrance gate, offering a dramatic expanse of rolling grassy meadows dotted with sprawling oak trees. The sparkling blue-green Guadalupe River serves as a mile and a half of the ranch's southern boundary and bubbling springs flow into beautiful Spring Branch Creek as it meanders through the property.

A field of Comanche Indian arrowheads testifies to a bygone culture that lived on the bountiful land. Chuck Knibbe recalls stories of his great, great-grandfather, Hans Heinrich Dietrich Knibbe of Biessendorf, Germany, who bought land along the Guadalupe for a dollar an acre to establish his 22,000-acre ranch near the present community of Spring Branch. The generally friendly Indians traded black bear skins and beaver pelts for eggs, milk and butter.

Archaeological exploration on the ranch indicates sites tucked along the shaded waterways of pre-historic nomadic Native American campgrounds dating from the Paleolithic to Late Archaic periods (8,000-500 B.C.). Numerous bison bones found at the base of the cliff overlooking one of the on-going digs reveals a bison kill site.

For more than 140 years, red, white-face Hereford cattle were the mainstay of the Knibbe Ranch. Today, however, the ranch produces "F-1 Tiger stripes," a hardy, first cross between purebred Hereford cattle and purebred Brahman cattle. The Knibbes have found the bred-in environmental adaptability, higher fertility and heat and disease resistance demonstrated by the F-1 female to be ideal for the Texas Hill Country, bringing an optimum price at market.

Five years ago, in order to broaden the ranch income base, the retired stock broker entered into a joint hospitality venture with the Destination Management Division of Marriott Rivercenter/Riverwalk of San Antonio to orchestrate ranch adventures for corporate and convention visitors, weddings and private events. A Texas-style veranda

surrounds Knibbe Halle, a 12,000 square foot air-conditioned country lodge built of recycled antique wood and corrugated steel from buildings originally found on the ranch. Large sliding barn doors on three sides of the building may be opened to bring in the gentle Texas breeze or closed to keep the warmth of a fire from the massive stone fireplace. Ranch offerings include a full-scale lighted rodeo arena and meadows bounded by the sparkling waters of oak-shaded Spring Branch Creek. Customized entertainment has included rodeos, balloon rides, music groups, team building activities, trail riding, fly-fishing and hunting. Guests can test their marksmanship on the skeet shooting range, experiment with the "atlatl" (the spear throwing weapon of pre-historic times), learn about the Texas Hill Country on a hayride or visit an active archaeological dig.

Wildlife thrives on this typical Hill Country ranch, where herds of White-tailed Deer, Axis Deer, feral hogs and Rio Grande Turkeys abound. Jackrabbits, cottontails, Red Foxes, Gray Foxes, raccoons, opossums and armadillos are typical sightings. The magnificent cypress trees that grace the Guadalupe River and the stately, moss-draped Spanish and Live Oaks and palmetto groves along the banks of Spring Branch Creek are the habitat of hawks, heron, kingfishers, ducks and songbirds.

Wildlife conservation and habitat management are natural priorities for the Knibbes, who play an ongoing role in the Spring Branch community. In 2005, the Comal-Guadalupe Soil and Water Conservation District honored Chuck Knibbe as District Winner for Outstanding Wildlife Conservation and for promotion of conservation activities.

Franz | Spring Branch Creek

Knibbe Ranch
10006 Spring Branch Road
Spring Branch, TX 78070
Toll Free: 877-6KNIBBE
Office: 830-885-7773
Fax: 830-885-7398
www.knibberanch.com

Photo courtesy of Sherwood Inkley

D. Robert Franz

A Kodak Brownie camera, backyard bird feeder and makeshift blind—together, these three items from Robert's childhood in Western Pennsylvania helped shape the direction this young man's life would ultimately follow. When others were out riding bikes and playing baseball, Robert admits to "spending hours in that blind happily snapping away." Fortunately, for those today who appreciate nature photography, his early interest took root and grew into a lifelong passion that has fostered a satisfying and very successful career.

With hundreds of publication credits to his name—including work printed in *National Geographic, Outdoor Life* and *Audubon*, among others—Robert (with his wife Lorri, also a talented photographer) had more than 650 images published in 47 countries last year alone. As further kudos, he was recently awarded a first place and received a "Highly Honored" mention in the 2004 Nature's Best International Photography Awards. With ongoing photography commissions across the globe, various writing assignments and a photo library containing more than 200,000 images, Robert's life is full indeed.

The gifted shooter believes a great wildlife photo must "clearly define the intended subject, eliminate visual clutter and, most importantly, tell the story of how the subject lives."

Cody, Wyoming
www.franzfoto.com

Franz | Bald Cypress along the Guadalupe River

Franz | Spider Webbing on Rattle Pod

Franz | Crayfish

Franz | Bold Jumper

Franz | Barred Owl

Franz | Pipevine Swallowtail on Buttercup

Franz | Blotched Water Snakes

Franz | Male Painted Bunting

Franz | Silvery Checkerspot

Franz | Columbine

Franz | Waterfall on Spring Branch Creek

Franz | Fern frond unfurling (species unknown)

Franz | Blacked-bellied Whistling Duck

About Red Creek Nature Ranch...

Illg | Spanish Dagger

Red Creek Nature Ranch has recently converted from a 95-year-old family working ranch that supplemented its income with hunting lease revenues to a property that focuses on the environment, seeking to provide a variety of experiences for the nature tourist. John Kothmann, with his sons Kevin and James, operates the 1,000-acre ranch where he has lived all his life, located near the headwaters of Red Creek outside of Junction, Kimble County, Texas.

Descendants of Heinrich and Katherine Kothmann, who were among the first 120 German settlers to make the rugged trip by covered wagon from Indianola on Matagorda Bay to New Braunfels and then onward to Fredericksburg, the family members have long acted as stewards for the lands they hold dear. Drawn by the desire to own land and raise large numbers of livestock, Heinrich purchased 640 acres to augment the 640 acres he received in the Fisher-Miller grant located between the Llano and San Saba Rivers. Despite a daunting presence of hostile Indians, the family moved to eastern Mason County in 1856. Starting over once again as pioneers in the wilderness, this time at the age of 58, the Kothmanns built a new home, raised their children and helped the older sons get started in the ranching business on their own. In 1909, their grandson, Eli Henry Kothmann, bought 6,000 acres for $3.00 per acre in eastern Kimble County between Junction and London. The southern portion of that purchase is now Red Creek Nature Ranch.

Located at the northwestern edge of the Edwards Plateau as it merges westward with the arid Trans-Pecos region and stretches north into the High Plains, the ranch offers richly diverse ecosystems. Pristine springs in "the land of living waters" seep from the limestone outcroppings to feed into Red Creek, a tributary to the Llano River. Native pecan and sycamore trees surround a grassy meadow where prehistoric native Americans once baked plant foods in rocky pits. Heat-fractured rocks and cooking debris, typical of ancient burned rock middens are mounded in the center of the clearing. Flint arrowheads, spearheads and tool fragments scattered about the site testify to more recent gatherings of nomadic Comanche, Apache or Kiowa tribes.

John Kothmann learned ranch management from his father in the days when Red Creek Nature Ranch specialized in cattle, sheep and mohair goats. While his dad was primarily a rancher and hunter, John credits an outstanding Boy Scout leader for inspiring his keen love of nature. Today the focus for the ranch is wildlife and land conservation. The Kothmanns monitor their deer population and carefully control selective hunting leases. Ashe Juniper cutting and burning is a ranch priority in order to protect and improve the water flow on the land. Cut trees are left in piles to provide shelter for nesting species. Deer and turkey feeders are strategically located while pastures dedicated to wheat and oats offer additional feed.

The dramatic contrast of hills and valleys, canyons and savannahs of Red Creek Nature Ranch offers exceptional opportunities for photographing wildlife, plants and scenery; as well as bird watching, hiking, biking and relaxing in a secluded, country environment. For the nature tourist, Red Creek Nature Ranch offers a choice of modern or rustic facilities for overnight, weekend or extended vacations for groups of up to 16 individuals.

lllg | Claret Cup Cactus

Red Creek Nature Ranch
John, Kevin and James Kothmann
P.O. Box 434
Junction, TX 76849
Phone: 325-475-2901
www.redcreeknatureranch.com
redcreek@ktc.com

lllg | Sunset over Red Creek Nature Ranch

Cathy Illg

Although Cathy always had a knack for snapping clever photos of the birds and the bees (initially with her Kodak Instamatic), it was marriage and the purchase of a 500mm lens that really got her to focus on wildlife photography as her life's work. Her husband, Gordon Illg, a dedicated backpacker, outdoorsman and professional photographer as well, introduced Cathy to the greater wonders of the wild where she was able to immerse herself in nature. With the acquisition of good, commercial equipment that gave her the tools to maximize her talents, Cathy was able to achieve the stunning and imaginative results she is recognized for today.

Cathy's award-winning work appears in nearly every major nature publication in North America. Her career soared to new heights when several of her photos were selected to grace the exteriors of a commercial airline fleet. And, as an adjunct to her career, she and Gordon conduct nature photography tours (under the name Adventure Photography) and have authored several books on the subject, the latest titled *Dynamic Wildlife Photography*.

Admitting that she is often attracted to places and species that others have passed by, Cathy explains that, "Every *thing* in nature, no matter how common or overlooked, has a story to tell and can play a central role in the creation of an exceptional photograph."

Lakewood, Colorado
www.advenphoto.com

Illg | Pocket Mouse with Prickly Pear Cactus

Illg | Immature True Bugs

Illg | Nine-banded Armadillo

IIIg | Eastern Cottontail

IIIg | Live Oak-Juniper Woodland

IIIg | Madrone Illuminated by Lightening

IIIg | Female Black-chinned Hummingbird

Illg | Male Pyrrhuloxia

Illg | Immature Long-horned Grasshopper

Illg | Texas Horned Lizard

Illg | Black Widow

About Annandale Ranch...

Perry | Male Painted Bunting

In the 1880's San Antonio attorney Lewis Florea began buying shares of stock in the Annandale Land and Cattle Company. By the end of the decade, he had bought out the other shareholders and continued to expand the ranch. Much of the property was purchased for 50 cents an acre at the courthouse auctions of Confederate land grants. Today fourth, fifth and sixth generation family members—the Cofer-Chapmans and McQuowns—own and manage the 10,000-acre property located in Uvalde County, just south of Concan, Texas.

Five miles of the Frio River and many caves that reach into the underground cavern system comprising the Edwards Aquifer make Annandale Ranch particularly vital to the region's ecological balance. The Frio Bat Cave, surrounded by the ranch, is the second largest bat population in the state and offers a unique ecosystem of its own. At twilight, an estimated 10 million bats pour forth—a dark ribbon of winged bodies—on their nightly foray. Fulfilling an important role in the control of pest insect populations, the small mammals consume tons of flying insects before swirling in a tornado-like formation back into their cavernous shelter just before dawn. Springtime migration brings more than 200 species of birds to the area, including raptors such as Red-tailed Hawks and Peregrine Falcons that feast on the bats as they emerge from the cave.

The land shelters abundant wildlife such as deer, Bobcats, Ringtails and Gray Foxes. A wide stretch of the Frio River, bordered by majestic cypress trees, creates a shaded haven for memorable family picnics. The nearby grove of trees, kept pristine and serene, offers prime nesting material for songbirds. Wild turkeys cut a pathway through a cedar break as they forage down to the clear blue river.

Annandale Ranch operates as a cattle, sheep and goat ranch and augments income through hunting leases and specialized eco-tourism opportunities, offering limited public access to parts of the property for birding and sunset bat viewing. Careful management of livestock through the generations has protected native grasses and forbs. The ranch actively engages in brush clearing and re-seeding through a contract with the National Resources

Conservation Service. In the winter, the ranch uses controlled burns on a pasture rotation program to help control brush undergrowth and kill Ashe Juniper seedlings.

Elevating land stewardship to paramount importance, the family has placed much of Annandale Ranch under a conservation easement, selling development rights on a large portion of the property to The Nature Conservancy, the Edwards Aquifer Authority and the San Antonio Water System. This Purchase of Development Rights agreement allows continued ranching and eco-tourism while preventing subdivision and commercial development. The family's vision includes educating people about the value of land and wildlife preservation.

United by their strong sense of family heritage, the descendants of Lewis and Eliza Florea desire to honor the legacy created for them more than 100 years ago by preserving the pristine beauty of Annandale Ranch. In the words of one family member, "The wide open spaces, clear waters of the Frio, and native wildlife are all gifts to us today from those who have gone before. It is not hard to imagine that our great, great-grandparents lived on this ranch and marveled at the abundant wildlife and beauty of the country. This is a gift that with careful planning will be passed on to future generations. Perhaps 100 years from now someone will have the opportunity to spot a Painted Bunting during a nature walk or discover Mountain Lion prints along the banks of the Frio."

Perry | Frio River

Annandale Ranch
466 Annandale Ranch Rd.
Sabinal, TX 78881
Office: 830-988-2202
Bill Cofer: 830-988-2864
Bruce McQuown: 830-988-2631

Phone for Bat Viewing:
Hill Country Nature Tours: 830-966-2320
www.hillcountryadventures.com

Perry | Bald Cypress-Sycamore Riparian Woodland

Al Perry

Al started snapping, developing and printing his own pictures as a young GI in the United States Army. After leaving the service, his camera remained an important part of his life. Pursuing a variety of opportunities over the next 27 years, the Mid-westerner eventually established himself as a successful shooter specializing in weddings and social events. Always drawn to the outdoors (Al grew up on the family farm), the working photographer finally traded I do's and wingdings for wildlife in 1998.

One of the award-winning shooter's favorite assignments was as a participating photographer in a British Broadcasting Corporation documentary on Sandhill and Whooping Cranes. Seeking a unique perspective, Al took wing with the big birds in his camera-equipped ultralight airplane. The dramatic and technically challenging footage generated on those flights continues to enjoy international exposure.

The respected photographer's images have been used by such organizations as the National Audubon Society, the National Wildlife Foundation, the International Crane Foundation and the Nebraska Bird Observatory.

And just what does it take to produce a great nature photo? Al responds, "The best require a photographer who starts with an appreciation of nature and is able to create an image that is technically accurate, artistically pleasing and most importantly, inspiring to the viewer."

Evansville, Indiana

Perry | Agave Leaves

Perry | Male Painted Bunting

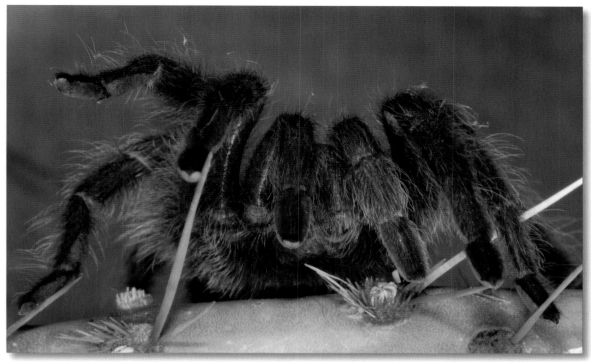

Perry | Texas Tan Tarantula

Perry | Frio River at Sunset

Perry | Northern Raccoon

Perry | Bald Cypress

Perry | Collared Peccary

Perry | Male Wild Turkeys

About Block Creek Natural Area...

Keeler | Cedar Elm Woodland

Block Creek Natural Area is a collaborative entry comprised of almost 900 acres located in Kendall County between Comfort and Fredericksburg, Texas off of Old Highway 9. The properties were once part of Hillingdon Ranch, founded by renowned architect Alfred Giles and named for his family home in Hillingdon, Middlesex, England. Giles immigrated to the United States in 1873, settling in San Antonio for health reasons. Unpretentious domestic residences, showy mansions, county courthouses, and commercial and institutional structures all over Texas and in parts of northern Mexico testify to Alfred Giles's restrained architectural simplicity. After 1885, Giles began purchasing land near Comfort, Texas. The ranch soon comprised 13,000 acres and produced horses, mules, registered Aberdeen Angus cattle, Angora goats and sheep. A founding member of the Texas Sheep and Goat Raisers Association, Giles instituted progressive land management practices that have been continued by his family to the present.

Carved from the past and surrounded by extended family properties, the Block Creek Natural Area has been cared for and loved by six generations of family members including David K. Langford, his wife Myrna, his cousin Milby Moore and their lifelong friends Sharron and Larry Jay. Ashe Juniper was cleared from the land before 1900 and the family continues a tradition of holistic range management. Rotational livestock grazing, exotic species control and maintaining deer within the carrying capacity of the habitat have allowed lush native grasses to thrive on the land, supporting a strong oak and native tree community. Springs flow year round and the crystal clear waters of Elm Bottom Creek bounce and sparkle down their rocky way to unite with the broad meander of Block Creek. Plentiful and diverse vegetation provides habitat for many species of resident and migratory wildlife.

Internationally recognized, award-winning wildlife photographer and writer David K. Langford began seriously photographing the land and wildlife after receiving his first 35mm camera as a wedding gift in 1967. An active supporter of the arts and conservation, Langford currently serves as Vice President Emeritus for the Texas Wildlife Association. Myrna also comes from a multi-generation family from nearby Comfort. A charter board member of the Hill Country Chapter of the Texas Master Naturalist program, she actively participates in the operation of the ranch.

Sharron Jay, Honorary Life Member of the Texas Wildlife Association, shares a lifelong passion for land stewardship and conservation with her husband Larry. The couple operates a first-class bed and breakfast on their property, which nestles comfortably beside a quiet spring-fed pond. Guests enjoy the wonders of Hill Country living—wide skies, brilliant stars and deep silence—away from the stresses and distractions of daily life.

For Milby Moore, caring for her horses and stewardship of her ranch are life callings. She never ceases to delight in the wonder of discovery—a newborn fawn, a hummingbird nest, a rummaging armadillo, a dew-filled dawn or a majestic sunset. Milby participates in hands-on management of her ranch almost every day of the year, and is also a Texas Master Naturalist.

With an eye to developing a photo tourism business, the partners have installed morning and evening photo blind settings, complete with water interests and feeders to attract birds and mammals. The lightweight camouflage-draped blinds are designed to offer portability and to avoid casting unwanted shadows.

Block Creek Natural Area beautifully reflects the concept of "land ethic" developed by Aldo Leopold, considered by many as the father of wildlife management: "Husbandry is the heart of conservation." (From *Land-Use and Democracy,* by Aldo Leopold, 1942)

Keeler | Spring-fed Creek

Block Creek Natural Area
Myrna and David K. Langford
P.O. Box 1059
Comfort, TX 78013
Phone: 830-995-2147
dkl@texas-wildlife.org
Milby Moore
Sharron and Larry Jay
Phone: 830-995-4174
sljay@gvtc.com

Keeler | Sunset in the Hill Country

Leo Keeler

While a youngster in southeast Arizona, Leo developed a love for the outdoors and all things wild. The pleasure he took in hunting, fishing and observing nature as a youth continued into his adult life. As an outdoorsman, Leo was often presented with opportunities and experiences within the natural world that he knew others would enjoy. Quite simply, he realized that photography gave him "a great way to share those experiences." It was a "natural" that he should become a professional wildlife photographer.

Today, Leo's photographic career is booming. Many of his images have been used in national advertising campaigns featured in such publications as *National Geographic, Newsweek, Alaska Magazine, Field and Stream* and *The Wall Street Journal*. He has also served as a photographic and wildlife consultant for several filmmakers.

Leo's success with nature photography led to his understanding of "how photography can change people's opinions and values of land and resources—how photos can become a powerful political tool." He and his wife Dorothy (also an accomplished photographer) are both environmentally active. Among other notable conservation-related accomplishments, the Keelers' inspiring photographs and efforts were instrumental in gaining protection for Alaska's McNeil River Refuge brown bear population and the Denali National Park Toklat wolf pack. They are founding members of the International League of Conservation Photographers.

Emigrant, Montana
www.akwildlife.com

Keeler | Oak Woodlands interspersed with Pastures

Keeler | Eastern Fence Lizard

Keeler | Red-tailed Hawk

Keeler | Spiny Softshell (turtle)

Keeler | Lace Cactus Flower

Keeler | Ringtail

Keeler | Spicebush Swallowtail (caterpillar)

Keeler | Green Kingfisher (female above, male below)

Keeler | Eastern Hognose Snake

About Flying A Ranch...

Vestal | Blackfoot Daisy (with some Bitterweed)

Intrigued by the creation and maintenance of suitable wildlife habitat, Albert B. Alkek, self-made oil millionaire, rancher, civic leader and philanthropist, imported animals from around the world for the ranch he purchased in 1958. Today the 9,200-acre Flying A Ranch, located in Bandera and Medina counties just south of Bandera, Texas, operates a successful cattle business in conjunction with a model program for hunters and wildlife enthusiasts.

Lush grasslands dotted with majestic oaks give way to shrublands dominated by Agarita and Texas Persimmon where descendants of Mr. Alkek's "exotics" thrive: Axis Deer and Black Buck Antelope from India, Sika from Manchuria and Formosa, Mouflon from Corsica and Sardinia, Fallow Deer from the Mediterranean, Aoudad from northern Africa and majestic Red Deer from Germany and Yugoslavia. Numerous creeks and springs feed into four lakes, offering plentiful water for wildlife and attracting an unusual number of waterfowl. A hand-cut native stone house dating from 1867, and a more recently built weekend family retreat nestled by the blue waters of an 18-acre lake on San Julian Creek, comprise the ranch headquarters.

Under the management of Charles Williams, Mr. Alkek's grandson, Flying A Ranch follows a habitat improvement plan with a priority focus on re-establishment of trophy quality White-tailed Deer. An extensive watering system with cisterns, pipelines and troughs has been installed in recent years to improve the distribution and availability of water for wildlife species and livestock. Free-choice feeders are available for the White-tailed Deer to supplement the native forage. The ranch utilizes carefully controlled livestock grazing to protect native plant growth and encourage diversity of plant species. Two full-time ranch biologists employ high-tech cameras to carefully monitor the deer population for selective harvesting and annual census data is collected for songbirds and plant species.

Embracing the environment of "Endangered Species," Flying A Ranch is actively working to create and maintain natural habitat. The ranch recently entered into a Safe Harbor Agreement and a Wildlife Stewardship Agreement with Environmental Defense as it focuses on restoring suitable low-shrub habitat for the endangered Black-capped Vireo. The small, olive-green and white songbirds nest in shrublands with broadleaf vegetation reaching

to the ground. The combination of overgrazing, brush clearing, and lack of fire in the recent past has dramatically reduced vireo habitat. Brown-headed Cowbirds, usually associated with livestock and farms, lay their eggs in other birds' nests, leaving the host bird to raise their young. This nest parasitism poses an additional strain on the fragile vireo population. Fragmentation due to urban and suburban development has also severely impacted the vireo. With the Black-capped Vireo in mind, Flying A Ranch is using prescribed burns and Ashe Juniper clearing along with the trapping of the parasitizing cowbirds in a 5,000-acre pasture. Call boxes are used to draw in vireos for nesting. Potential habitat for the endangered Golden-cheeked Warbler is also located in this area of the ranch.

Education is a priority for Flying A Ranch, which participates in the Edwards Plateau Rio Grande Turkey Project, working with the Department of Wildlife and Fisheries Sciences at Texas A&M University. The ranch hosts college field trips from Texas State, Tarleton State, Texas Tech and other state institutions. College interns have the opportunity to earn credits in ranch management and environmental development while working with the ranch staff during the summer and fall.

Flying A Ranch features the warm and welcoming Lodge on San Julian Creek, a first class bed and breakfast facility for visitors to the Texas Hill Country. A limestone lodge and cottages with wide Texas-style covered porches offer ample opportunity to sit, relax and enjoy the outdoors. In the evenings, a stone fire-pit provides a friendly campfire setting to take the chill off the cool Hill Country dusk. Guests can enjoy the flowing San Julian Creek or take a wildlife tour and learn about the animals, birds and habitats on the ranch. Guided hunts, fishing and photography opportunities are also available.

Vestal | Live Oak

Flying A Ranch
The Lodge on San Julian Creek
1919 State Highway 173 South
Bandera, Texas 78003
Phone: 866-796-4750
www.flyingAranch.net, www.SJCreek.net

Vestal | Sunset over Flying A Ranch

Gary Vestal

Gary has been photographing nature for three decades. From the beginning, the assignments he is most passionate about are the ones where subjects are explored intensely over multi-year periods. His subject matter can be as varied as documenting (up close) the fascinating life cycles of Monarch and Swallowtail butterflies to challenging charging tigers in the wilds of Asia. Countless images are patiently captured over time, building compelling visual records of his themes. Needless to say, this depth of dedication keeps Gary in the field nine days out of ten.

Working through large commercial photography agencies, Gary's images have become a staple in the corporate and advertising worlds. Additional exposure for the artist has come with the publication of his photos in such important periodicals as *National Geographic, Audubon* and *Sierra Magazine*. His work has been repeatedly recognized by his peers throughout his long career.

Today, Gary is pioneering a technique where multiple images shot sequentially are merged into one panoramic whole. The dramatic results can superbly illustrate movement, behaviors or seasonal changes on a single photographic panel.

Portland, Oregon

Vestal | Gulf Fritillary on Firewheel

Vestal | Male Vermilion Flycatcher

Vestal | Male Wild Turkey

Vestal | White-tailed Deer

Vestal | Pink Evening Primrose

Vestal | Red-eared Slider

Vestal | Lindheimer Prickly Pear Flower

Vestal | Rio Grande Leopard Frog (tadpole)

Vestal | Male American Goldfinch

About JSB Ranch...

Richardson | Agarita

JSB Ranch wraps around a sparkling stretch of the Nueces River not far from the headwaters near Barksdale, Texas, in Real County. The property has been in family ownership since the 1930's. Dr. Homer Grant Boren, a renowned American practicing dentistry in the resort community of Torreón, Mexico, purchased the beautiful Texas Hill Country property in order to diversify his holdings and to raise his young son back in his native Texas. Born and raised on the property, James Sandy Boren, Sr. passed on his love of the land and the wildlife it harbors to his own children and grandchildren.

The JSB Ranch, formerly known as the Boren Ranch, boasts a history of managed cattle grazing, Boer goat production and at one time, a large Angora goat population. Spring-fed lakes supplement the river flow to offer unspoiled wildlife habitat to a wide range of birds, reptiles and small mammals. An early morning ramble through the ranch might turn up a scampering jackrabbit, a darting fox, Coyote or roadrunner, a foraging armadillo or a pack of feral hogs on the rampage. White-tailed Deer feed quietly among the trees, ready to flash the white underside of their stubby tails as they bolt to nearby cover. Large-antlered bucks proudly display their multi-pointed racks while does watch over their spotted fawns. A Great Horned Owl swoops to capture a field mouse, creating a screeching ruckus as he returns to roost from nocturnal adventures.

The rocky ranch road twists and turns through fields dotted with Texas Mountain Laurel and Prickly Pear Cactus, which bursts forth in the spring with a breath-taking display of rose-like yellow, pink and red blooms. A high ridge reveals dramatic westward views with the promise of stunning purple-pink sunsets. Pecan trees mark the river bottomland that yields evidence of an ancient Native American camping ground. The archeological mounds create a mystical link to an era of pristine wilderness and nomadic tribes. There the clear, cool spring water whirls and splashes across the white-rocked riverbed, while a gentle breeze whispers through the trees.

JSB Ranch is a spiritual place where Dayna Boren Cartwright, ranch owner and daughter of James Sandy Boren, Sr., can reconnect with her roots and feel closest to God. To escape the stresses of daily life, she heads for the scenic

route to her beloved ranch. It is the quintessential Hill Country drive, offering stunning vistas, hidden canyons, cloistered valleys and lush grazing lands. An avid supporter of wildlife preservation and habitat protection for endangered species, Dayna is the owner of Cartwright Media Group, Inc.—a media buying and marketing firm—and is the publisher of *Travelhost Magazine of the Texas Hill Country*. She has been involved in journalism, marketing and media sales for two decades and serves in many volunteer capacities including several current board positions that include the Greater Boerne Chamber of Commerce, the ICF Hill Country Advisory Board and the National Advisory Board for Travelhost Corporation.

To protect and preserve the heritage she treasures, Dayna Boren Cartwright works with the ranch's second-generation foreman, J.B. "Bubby" Hutto. The owner of a neighboring ranch, Hutto grew up on the property and has worked with the family for several decades. The family would one day like to operate the JSB Ranch as a non-profit foundation that allows school children and their families the opportunity to experience nature. The Cartwrights plan to introduce nature photography and bird watching programs to the ranch in 2007, with the goal of adding lodging in gradual stages over the next several years.

Richardson | Nueces River

JSB Ranch
Dayna Boren Cartwright
215 W. Bandera Rd. #114-118
Boerne, TX 78006
Phone: 210-365-6452
daynacartwright@yahoo.com

Richardson | Woodlands

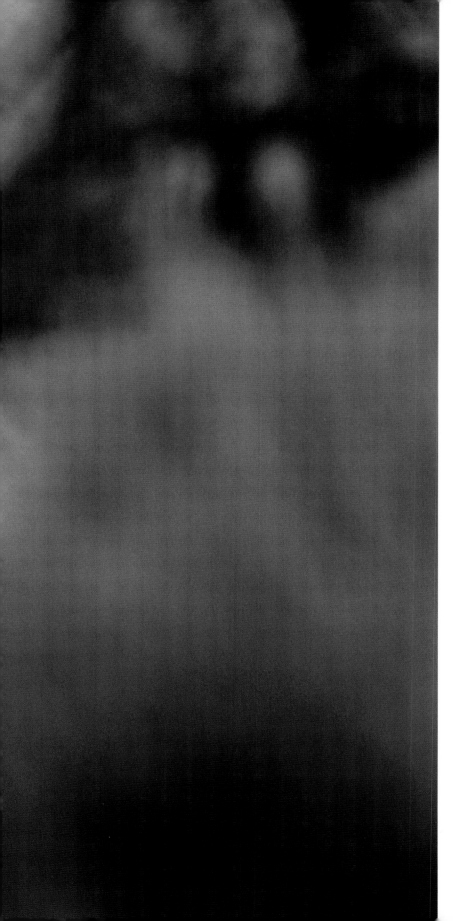

Lynda Richardson

"My dad's love of taking pictures and the gift of a Kodak Instamatic when I was in third grade," is what Lynda would tell you spurred a passion for photography that continues to this day. As a working professional for the past 20-plus years, this talented photographer began her career handling assignments for the *Associated Press, U.S. News, Time* and other prestigious, national news outlets before making the commitment to focus exclusively on wildlife and environmental photojournalism—a commitment made when she realized that nature was where her "heart" was.

Was it a good choice? *Nature's Best* magazine thought so when Lynda was recognized as one of the top outdoor women photographers. Today, the energetic shooter finds the time to teach and write while tackling projects across the globe for the likes of the Smithsonian, National Wildlife and The Nature Conservancy. With her "beyond the call of duty" work ethic, unique perspectives and high degree of technical expertise it's no surprise her award-winning work in the field attracts the national and international audience that it does.

And what makes a truly great nature photograph? Lynda unhesitatingly volunteers, "It takes your breath away when you see it, it surprises you, or it teaches you something about the subject—preferably, all three."

Richmond, Virginia
www.lyndarichardson.com

Richardson | Black-tailed Jackrabbit

Richardson | Pecan

Richardson | Red-eared Slider (turtle)

Richardson | Male Blue Grosbeak

Richardson | Mayfly with Mealy Sage

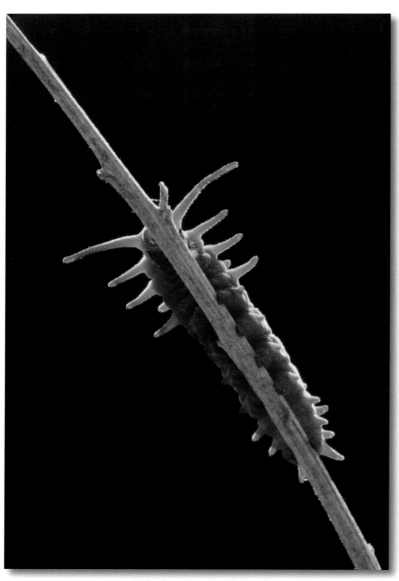

Richardson | Pipevine Swallowtail (caterpillar)

Richardson | White-footed Mouse

Richardson | Cinnamon Teal

Richardson | Green Algae

About KKW Game & Cattle, LLC...

Welling | Nursery Web Spider on Lace Cactus

KKW Game & Cattle, LLC honors a heritage of wildlife preservation. The property comprises 5,500 contiguous acres in Bandera, Medina and Bexar counties and is located just north of Helotes, Texas. Descendants of famed Texas Ranger and rancher Captain Charles A. Schreiner and rancher Ike West, both Kittie Nelson Ferguson and her daughter Kittie West Ferguson Hughes strive to carefully maintain a balance between cattle production, exotic game management and wildlife preservation.

Modern grazing strategies and de-stocking have allowed the native vegetation to thrive. Long-term control of invader species, such as Ashe Juniper, water development and preservation of pristine areas characterize a healthy ecosystem that is evolving to its natural potential. Magnificent oak trees grace gently rolling hills, offering sweeping vistas across open rangeland, lush with native grasses and dotted with Texas Agarita and Mountain Laurel shrubs. The headwaters of San Geronimo Creek spring from limestone outcroppings on the property and flow through a series of man-made lakes. Stock tanks offer additional water sources and associated wetlands.

The family has worked closely with the Texas Parks & Wildlife Department and private consultants to manage the native White-tailed Deer and exotic species on the ranch. KKW Game & Cattle personnel regularly conduct spotlight and aerial helicopter counts to determine appropriate harvesting quotas. The ranch also monitors non-game wildlife species such as fox, Coyote, Ringtail and raccoon.

Wildlife and livestock receive further support through corn and protein supplement feeding. Bat boxes, planned placement of brush piles, slash retention, creation of specific shelters for quail and the practice of stacking posts in teepees offer supplemental shelter for wildlife. The ranch has developed shallow wetlands and ponds, along with wells to supplement the many natural springs on the property. Careful long-term planning allows KKW Game & Cattle to achieve livestock grazing objectives while supporting exceptional wildlife. Grazing management techniques include rotating livestock to ensure periodic rest for pastures, following recommended conservative

stocking rates, and deferring grazing for a year. Emphasis is placed on controlling the grazing and browsing pressure from White-tailed Deer and exotic ungulates, such as Axis Deer. In addition, the ranch has initiated an aggressive program to control native and exotic predator species such as Coyotes, feral hogs, raccoons, and wild dogs, along with fire ants and cowbirds.

KKW Game & Cattle offers customized hunting, fishing and recreational opportunities. A stone lodge and guesthouse provide deluxe accommodations, while gourmet cuisine and unique amenities enhance the beautiful natural environment. Guests can hunt native White-tailed Deer or quail, fish for perch or Large-mouth Bass in the well-stocked lakes or target exotic game such as Axis and Fallow Deer, Blackbuck Antelope, Sika and Auodad. For the nature tourist, guided game drives and photo safaris compliment activities such as hiking and bird watching.

The opportunity to work with a photographer of Dave Welling's caliber was a richly rewarding experience for Kittie West Hughes. Nocturnal adventures chasing skunks with spotlights and the discovery of the importance of snakes to the avid wildlife photographer were competition highlights. She learned how to call in birds and spent hours taking her own photographs with expert guidance. From a commercial perspective, the Pro-Tour offered new insights for the ranch's blossoming nature tourism business.

Welling | Sunset

KKW Game & Cattle, LLC
300 Austin Hwy, Suite 150
San Antonio, TX 78209
Phone: 210-930-7990
www.kkwgameandcattle.com

Welling | Oak Woodland

Dave Welling

After two decades as a professional wildlife photographer, Dave admits his most memorable assignment was photographing the mountain gorillas living in the Virungas National Forest, Zaire, Africa. He recalls, "Being in close proximity to these magnificent creatures was simply incredible—made more so by the knowledge that their very existence is tenuous. As if to reinforce this, I learned a male silverback that featured prominently in many of my photographs was killed by poachers shortly after the assignment ended." But then he adds, "Maybe my images can help preserve and protect the threatened in nature."

With numerous publishing credits under his belt (his images have appeared in such notable venues as *National Geographic, Audubon, Outdoor Photographer* and *World Wildlife Fund*), Dave has also received recognition with first place awards and multiple honorable mentions in the prestigious BBC Wildlife Photographer of the Year and the Nature's Best International Photography Awards. He also finds time to share his photography expertise as a writer and teacher.

Asked if wildlife photography required hard work, Dave quickly replies, "No assignment is 'easy' if you want good images. After spending days in a blind hoping a colorful bird would be attracted to some brilliant Opuntia blossoms, a Golden-fronted Woodpecker landed right where I wanted and began eating the pollen. It was more than I ever hoped for."

Canoga Park, California
www.agpix.com/davewelling

Welling | Female Nursery Web Spider

Welling | Live Oak

Welling | Common Earth Snake

Welling | Giant Redheaded Centipede

Welling | Texas Rat Snake

Welling | Carolina Wren

Welling | Flower Scarabs on Lindheimer Prickly Pear Flower

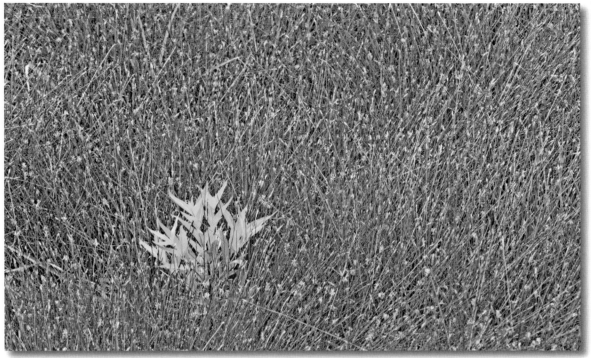

Welling | Young Buttonbush surrounded by Spikesedge

Welling | Red-tailed Hawk

About Krause Ranch...

Schulz | Riparian Woodland

The West Fork of the Frio River and several spring-fed creeks wind through the 2,000-acre Krause Ranch located near Leakey, Texas, in Real County. In recent years, extensive clearing of Ashe Juniper, along with careful wildlife management, have returned tall grasses and clustered oak mottes to their native state of abundance, thus restoring the life-giving flow of continuous natural springs throughout the property. Located in the area once famed as Pearl Beer's "land of eleven hundred springs," the Krause Ranch acts as a sieve, funneling rainfall and runoff deep into the earth where it can be stored in limestone caverns.

Church Spring, the largest of the springs, is presently under study by the Texas Parks & Wildlife Department and the Nueces River Authority. Characterized as one of "Texas Finest Treasures," Church Spring pours forth from the limestone outcropping into a tree-shaded pool lined with ancient ferns, mountain laurels and leafy shrubs. A stately stone in the middle of the pristine stream creates an altar-like effect while a fallen tree that spans the creek provides a sheltered pew to capture a mystical moment. The spring is home to rare bullnose minnows and an unusual species of flesh-toned salamanders.

On the opposite side of the mountain, a sister spring flows from honeycombed rock into a sinkhole, a cavernous body of underground water known as Englishmen's Well. Divers and a reel truck with wire line have failed to plumb the depth of the crystal clear waters. Petrified coral and prehistoric clam beds testify to ancient geographic upheaval.

Passionate about land, water and wildlife preservation, ranch owner Gary Krause helped initiate the Volunteer Testing Program of the TNRCC (Texas National Resource Conservation Commission) and has served as one of the certified water testers for the state. Conservation and education are primary goals for Gary and Gwen Krause. As a child accompanying his USDA Field Agent father as he worked Hill Country ranches, six-year-old Gary announced, "I'm going to own my own ranch so I can go whenever I want." By 1983 the owner of Intercontinental Training, an

international management training and consulting company, began purchasing the properties that today comprise Krause Ranch.

Currently the land is used for cattle production and recreational hunting. Faithful workers Salvador and Manuel Garcia-Centeño have played an indispensable role in the reclamation and improvement of the land. From brush management, to fence building, to constructing a stone house around an old stone water tank, the hard-working brothers have made the ranch their home.

Krause Ranch limits human interaction on the property and carefully manages grazing and hunting. Wildlife management objectives focus on conservation of native species and balancing the free-grazing exotic wildlife. Programs under development include habitat protection, animal population control, provision of supplemental water sources and feed supplements.

A lifelong goal for Gary Krause has been to leverage his efforts by educating the general population about the importance of conservation practices and the value of preserving native Texas habitat. To that end, the Krauses are working through lawyers to establish a conservation easement to ensure that the land will always be preserved as a natural wildlife habitat—free from land fragmentation. Protection of the aquatic habitat is of utmost concern, as is the goal of keeping the West Fork of the Frio River private and non-navigable. Working with other local landowners, state and federal agencies and local law officials, Gary Krause has taken a leading roll in land preservation through control of trespassing and pollution as a result of human activities.

Schulz | Live Oak

Krause Ranch
Gary and Gwen Krause
P.O. Box 1187
Leakey, TX 78873
garykrause@garykrause.com
gwen@garykrause.com

Schulz | Hill Country Oak Woodland

Florian Schulz

From his first snapshots of small backyard lizards (taken with a used Praktika camera at age 12) to his dramatic images of a charging Black Rhino in southern Africa (where he barely escaped with his life) and beyond, Florian's passion for wildlife photography remains a lifelong focus. This passion grew out of the talented shooter's deep respect for all things in nature and a desire to preserve the endangered in the wild. As he explains, "I've succeeded if my photographs evoke an emotional response in the viewer and then make the viewer care more about the subject."

The award winning photojournalist, conservationist and author is one of the founding members of the International League of Conservation Photographers and is currently involved in several environmentally directed efforts—the most notable being the massive Yellowstone to Yukon project involving multiple states and territories in the United States and Canada. His recently released book *Yellowstone to Yukon: The Freedom to Roam* was named by Independent Publisher as one of the ten outstanding books of the year.

When Florian approaches an outdoor assignment, he strives to capture the ecosystem in its entirety. As he relates, "I'm happy if my work helps others experience the mood of a total environment through the images of diverse animal life and vegetation."

Germany
www.visionsofthewild.com

Schulz | Yellow-throated Vireo

Schulz | Krause Ranch Vista

Schulz | Chatterbox Orchid with Maidenhair Fern

Schulz | Baird's Rat Snake

Schulz | Eastern Fox Squirrel

Schulz | Male Vermilion Flycatcher

Schulz | Common Raven

Schulz | Greater Roadrunner

About Los Madrones...

Lee | Antelope Horn Milkweed

The Mike Murphy and Bert Von Roemer properties form a combined entry of 800 acres located off Hamilton Pool Road in Dripping Springs, Travis County, Texas. Little Bee Creek runs through both properties and there are several spring-fed lakes. The high-fenced Von Roemer property has been stocked with exotic game, including Black Buck Antelope, Elk and Axis Deer and is associated with the Serengeti Foundation, a non-profit organization promoting environmental and conservation issues. Through the foundation, Bert Von Roemer, the owner of an international coffee trading company, oversees land conservation projects in California, Montana and Texas. The Serengeti Foundation also aids in fundraising for Elephant Nature Park, a refuge for rescued elephants in northern Thailand.

When he was 14 years old, Mike Murphy moved with his family to Los Madrones, a ranch they had purchased in 1966. Inspired by the land he loves, Mike pursued a degree in photojournalism at Ohio University and the University of Texas at Austin followed by a career in journalism. Today the Photography Editor for *Texas Highways* lives on the ranch with his pediatrician wife, Julie DeWette-Murphy and their children Michaela and Nicholas. Through research for *Texas Highways*, Murphy began to focus on the habitat and environmental concerns related to Los Madrones. He worked with Selah, Bamberger Ranch Preserve on an article for the magazine and attended seminars, covering topics such as creek-side protection, brush control and the importance of Ashe Juniper removal to improve and protect natural water sources. As goals for the future of the ranch began to crystallize, Mike in 2000 converted Los Madrones from a cow and calf operation to a wildlife management property.

Ashe Juniper clearing has helped return portions of the dramatically beautiful property to a state of natural abundance. Tall native grasses flank the gravel road into the property. A gentle rise suddenly drops downward to reveal a breathtaking view of the creek below and shadowed hills beyond. The family's native stone home offers a panorama of the surrounding countryside and gardens are planted to attract birds and mammals.

The Murphys keep a daily log of wildlife sightings and management activities. Songbirds are plentiful and it is particularly exciting to spot a Golden-cheeked Warbler during its nesting time from March until late June. The small

black and white songbirds with bright yellow cheeks are an endangered species whose entire nesting range is currently confined to habitat in 33 counties in central Texas. The warblers are dependent on mature Ashe Juniper for fine bark strips used in their nest construction. While nests may be located in various species of trees such as Texas Oak, Live Oak, and Cedar Elm, all nests contain strips of Ashe Juniper bark woven together with spider webs. Golden-cheeked Warblers forage and nest in vigorously defended "territories" of five to 20 acres per pair, and males are known to return to the same territory from year to year. Selective Ashe Juniper removal and trapping of the brood parasitic Brown-headed Cowbirds is particularly important to the survival of the Golden-cheeked Warblers.

The ranch priority is the restoration of habitat for Rio Grande Turkey, Northern Bobwhite Quail, White-tailed Deer, song birds and small mammals. Supplemental feed is offered turkeys and quail, and predator management has been a focused effort. Bat and birdhouses are strategically positioned to further encourage the expanding bird population that is carefully catalogued in an annual spring census.

Looking to the future, Mike Murphy is particularly pleased that Los Madrones is located along the newly established Heart of Texas Trail for wildlife viewing. Designed to encourage nature tourism, the wildlife trails of Texas promote economic development and build public support for conservation of wildlife and habitats for present and future generations. The Murphy family plans to utilize photography blinds to offer nature photography opportunities to the public. Development of a lodge or bed and breakfast facilities will augment wildlife viewing and nature study.

Lee | Texas Oaks in Live Oak-Juniper Woodland Matrix

Los Madrones
Mike A. Murphy
19300 Hamilton Pool Road
Dripping Springs, TX 78620

Phone: 512-264-1741
mike@losmadrones.com
Bert Von Roemer
www.SerengetiUSA.com

Lee | Scattered Live Oaks

Jess Lee

As a member of a ranching family living in the foothills of the Sierra Nevada Mountains, a young Jess Lee spent a lot of time roaming the outdoors with camera in hand. Later, his skills as a shooter were further honed during his service as a military reconnaissance photographer. Dividing the next 30 years between a career in the communications industry and handling outside photographic assignments, Jess transitioned in 1999 into the respected, full-time professional wildlife photographer he is today.

Based near Yellowstone Park and the magnificent Tetons, this photographer might never need to leave his backyard to find inspiring subject matter. He admits, "I may live in the beautiful Rockies with grizzlies and other big mammals but land does not have to include herds of buffalo or a tall, pointed mountain with snow on it to be pretty." In search of the special, Jess keeps his cameras on the road (and off) devoting more than 200 days each year in the field photographing the beauty of nature.

Many of his impressive images have appeared in such notable publications as *Paris Match, National Geographic, Wilderness, Sports Afield* and *Sierra Magazine.* Between his work on two books and ongoing shooting assignments, Jess still finds time to share his expertise with others through workshops and tours.

Coltman, Idaho
www.jessleephotos.com

Lee | Lindheimer Prickly Pear in the Rain

Lee | Female Black-chinned Hummingbird

Lee | Male Northern Bobwhite

Lee | Male Golden-cheeked Warbler

Lee | Turkey Vultures

Lee | Gray Fox

Lee | Little Bluestem with Scattered Oaks

Lee | Sunset

Lee | Forest Tent Caterpillar on Vervain

About Northrup Pipe Creek Ranch...

Sloat | Madrone

During the Depression years, Preston Gaines Northrup was a railroad man, buying and leasing 20-mile swaths of land for railroad right-of-ways, while retaining ownership of the mineral rights. In 1936, he purchased his dream ranch in the Texas Hill Country. Northrup's 5,000-acre property located in Bandera, Kerr and Kendall counties near Pipe Creek, Texas, is a slice of paradise. Rocky ridgetops reveal dramatic vistas of rolling hills beyond— stretching in a blue-green blanket eastward to greet the morning sunrise and westward to magnificent sunsets. Hilltops give way to deep valleys and tree-lined waterways. The headwaters of Pipe Creek burble forth from the ground and seep from the surrounding limestone outcroppings before flowing southwestward into the Medina River. Year-round springs feed eight lakes. The road winds down into the valley where cattle and horses graze in the pastures.

Concerned with the environmental integrity of the property under his stewardship, Northrup structured a system of lakes and pastures to optimize his cattle business while protecting wildlife habitats. In the 1980's Lynn and Jane Northrup purchased the ranch. They continued to improve the land with the same passionate commitment to responsible land management shared with Preston and his wife Gretchen. For the past 25 years the family has worked with the local Natural Resources Conservation Service (NRCS) and the Soil and Water Conservation District under an approved Conservation Plan for balanced grazing, managed Ashe Juniper, prescribed burning and appropriate deer harvesting. Work is underway to protect and improve vegetation along creek beds. Over the last 20 years the Northrup Pipe Creek Ranch has worked closely with the Botany Department at Howard Payne University to collect information on hundreds of plant species.

In addition to abundant wildlife and game, the ranch offers excellent habitat conducive to three endangered species: the Golden-cheeked Warbler, the Black-capped Vireo and the Tobush Fish-hooked Cactus. Realizing that successful management requires sound decisions and a holistic world view, the family has turned their attention to environmental concepts proposed by Rhodesia-born Allan Savory and his Center for Holistic Resource Management. According to the model, decision makers simultaneously consider economic, social and environmental consequences, both short and long term, emphasizing land management practices that mimic nature.

Fourth generation family members Ben Eldredge and Kate Northrup Summers live on the property, attending to day-to-day management. The Northrup and Eldredge family members are unified by a desire to protect the land from development and fragmentation and have recently filed for the NRCS Grassland Reserve Program to ensure that Northrup Ranch will always be protected. Wildlife diversity, habitat protection and land conservation remain top priorities. The ranch has recently obtained organic certification and plans are under consideration to develop organic production for area farmers' markets—encouraging the practice of buying locally.

For the hunter or nature lover, Northrup Pipe Creek Ranch offers private ranch vacations, weekend getaways, corporate retreats, special event hosting and exclusive hunting trips. Nature photographers find abundant opportunities to capture the perfect shot from specialized photoblinds. A modernized Hill Country lodge, built in the early 1900's from stones quarried on the property, features views of the surrounding hills and is available for groups of six to ten individuals. Hunting opportunities include White-tailed Deer, feral hogs and Rio Grande Turkeys. Clear, spring-fed lakes offer catch-and-release fishing, canoeing, swimming and paddle boating. Miles of hiking and biking trails hug the high ridges before winding 1,000 feet down to the valley floor. Nature lovers may also enjoy guided trail rides, birding and wildlife viewing.

Sloat | Walking stick on Agarita

Northrup Pipe Creek Ranch
Ben Eldredge/Kate Northrup Summers
1673 New Northrup Ranch Road
P.O. Box 63356
Pipe Creek, Texas 78063
Phone: 830-535-4024
www.pipecreekranch.com

Mike Sloat

As a decorated 36-year career military pilot, current FAA safety specialist and avid motorcyclist, Mike wouldn't seem to fit your stereotypical profile of an acclaimed wildlife photographer—but he is. Since age 15, the year he started flying, Mike would pack an old Kodak box camera and snap black and whites of any and all things he came across, whether airborne or on the ground. Over the years, he has continued to hone his photographic skills (along with upgrading his equipment). Today, he is recognized as one of Texas' premier shooters.

Mike's work has been featured in such notable publications as *Texas Highways, Nature Photography, Texas Parks & Wildlife* and *Travel Host* magazine. He often journeys out of state to locations in Alaska, Wyoming, Colorado and New Mexico to capture his images and prides himself on the fact that "all of the animals featured (in his photos) are wild, in natural settings, and not tamed, on lease or from game farms."

And how does Mike define photographic success? With thought he responds, "A great picture will capture the viewers and take them to a place they have been or wish they could go. It will make them feel the warmth of the sun, smell the salt spray blowing off an ocean wave or hear the call of the eagle soaring above."

Fort Worth, Texas
www.txsoutdoorphotography.com

Sloat | Male Indigo Bunting

Sloat | Lindheimer Prickly Pear

Sloat | Fragrant Mimosa

Sloat | Rough Green Snake

Sloat | Prickly Poppy

Sloat | Texas Spiny Lizard

Sloat | Maidenhair Fern (L), Southern Shield Fern (R)

Sloat | House Finch (female above, male below)

About Peaceful Springs Nature Preserve, LLC...

Ulrich | Maidenhair Fern

Peaceful Springs Nature Preserve, LLC covers 530 acres of untouched wilderness, surrounded on three sides by more than 3,000 acres belonging to the U.S. Fish and Wildlife Balcones Canyonlands National Wildlife Refuge. The Preserve is located in southeastern Burnet county, northwest of Austin, Texas. Owners David and Cynthia Castleberry have operated the property as a family cattle ranch for more than 25 years and in 1999 began a Wildlife Management Plan. As a youngster, David spent many hours learning wilderness survival and the secrets of flora and fauna from his Native American Comanche grandfather. The retired Marine spends the majority of his time exploring every inch of the Hill Country property he loves, finding peace and healing in communion with nature.

Steep canyons and rolling hills offer breathtaking views of the blue-gray hills beyond. Thick woodlands, including a dense grove of native Texas Walnut trees, grow along the creek and lake edges. Located in the recharge zone for the Northern Edwards Aquifer, Peaceful Springs Nature Preserve, LLC plays a vital role in watershed protection. In the recharge zone, porous and permeable Edwards Limestone is exposed at the surface, providing a direct path for water to reach the underground artesian zone. Streams and rainfall percolate directly into the underground water system through fractures, sinkholes and caves.

Plentiful seeps and springs on the property feed perennial creeks and four ponds. Cabin Spring burbles and flows into a series of three ponds creating a haven for water creatures, birds and animals. A possibly new species of salamander is under scrutiny and the Castleberrys have discovered an unusual small snake that seems to live underwater, rarely surfacing. Upon removal from the water, the small, foot-long creature promptly curls into a roll.

Peaceful Springs Nature Preserve, LLC is currently building a pavilion that includes handicap access to picnic and gathering areas, a kitchen and restroom facilities. An auxiliary well and stone amphitheater will complete the improvements located along the shores of the Catfish Pond, a large lake stocked with enormous catfish. There the Castleberrys envision scout troops, handicapped children, birders and non-profit groups will gather for specialized studies and exploration. Edible and medicinal plants, wildlife habits and lifecycles, and wilderness survival are a sampling of topics. Nature photography workshops and tours are offered along with guided birding and wildlife viewing excursions. A charming cabin on the property is available for quiet retreats, offering time-out from the stresses of life and an opportunity for quiet reflection and discovery.

Because the Preserve has not been hunted for more than 30 years, animals feel safe and do not fear the presence of man. Diverse ecosystems on the property provide natural habitat and opportunity for study of songbirds such as endangered Golden-cheeked Warblers and Black-capped Vireos, a wide variety of native Texas mammals (including Bobcats and Mountain Lions) and countless varieties of snakes. Rattlesnake Canyon located in one corner of the property is a deep ravine with a large rattlesnake den. Someday David Castleberry hopes to offer access to the dramatic site for viewing and study.

The family is in the process of implementing a ten-year plan, which includes an Ultra Low Density Conservation Development. The minimum impact development for 12 housing sites will require utilization of "green" building materials and practices. The remainder of the land will be held in a Conservation Easement, giving homeowners access to a limited area of the Preserve. Peaceful Springs Nature Preserve, LLC will operate as a non-profit entity designed to protect the property and to support scientific and environmental research and education.

Ulrich | Vervain

Peaceful Springs Nature Preserve, LLC
David and Cynthia Castleberry
P.O. Box 640
Liberty Hill, TX 78642
Phone: 512-355-3111
Fax: 512-355-3223
www.peacefulspringsnp.com

Ulrich | Early Morning Light

Ulrich | Texas Spiny Lizard

Tom Ulrich

Tom's career as a professional photographer evolved three decades ago from his earlier occupation as a high school biology teacher. His first photographic efforts were used as visuals to support his classes' curricula. It wasn't long however before Tom's avocation as wildlife photographer grew into the permanent and successful vocation he is respected for today.

With more than 350,000 images in his ever-growing portfolio, Tom's works regularly show up on the pages of such prestigious publications as *National Geographic, Life, Audubon* and *National Wildlife.* He has also found the time to publish seven nature books of his own including *Mammals of the Canadian Rockies, Once Upon a Frame, Photo Pantanal* and *Mt. Reynolds: The Story.* Tom, still the teacher, also enjoys leading groups on photographic tours across the globe and conducting seminars and workshops at prominent United States universities.

From his first place ranking in the 1987 British Broadcasting Corporation International Photographer of the Year competition to the receipt of the recent 2005 North American Nature Photography Association's Fellow Award, Tom continues to be recognized as a gifted professional. "The awards are nice," Tom admits, "but when someone sees one of my images then says 'Wow, how did you do that?' I know I did my job."

West Glacier, Montana
www.tomulrichphotos.com

Ulrich | Common Whitetail Dragonfly

Ulrich | Great Blue Heron

Ulrich | Bluets

Ulrich | Lace Cactus

Ulrich | Male Ruby-throated Hummingbird

Ulrich | White-footed Mouse

Ulrich | Striped Bark Scorpion

Ulrich | Checkered Garter Snake

About Petersen Ranch...

Fitzgerald | Misty Morning Sunrise

A commitment to balance wildlife preservation with sound economics drives Bob and Cindy Petersen's carefully designed management program for the 800-acre property they purchased in 1999. Petersen Ranch, located in Kendall County between Blanco and Luckenbach, Texas, suffered from heavy grazing by cattle and goats and an overpopulation of White-tailed Deer. Bob, a lifelong wildlife enthusiast, immediately began working to restore the property, establishing a program with Texas Parks & Wildlife Department (TPWD) and five adjacent ranches to monitor and control the deer population. Next he formed a project team with Environmental Defense, TPWD, The Nature Conservancy and the U.S. Fish and Wildlife Service (USFWS).

Located in the upper reaches of the Blanco River watershed, the rugged Petersen Ranch displays an incredible diversity of plant life not often seen on Hill Country ranches. Upper elevations feature ridge-top savannah pastures of tall native grasses, wildflowers and broad leaf plants dotted with stately Live Oaks and several species of flowering trees such as Texas Redbud, Texas Buckeye, Mexican Plum and rare Blanco Crabapple. The rolling ridgetops give way to heavily forested hillsides covered with Escarpment Black Cherry, Spanish Oak and Lacy Oak trees. Rainwater, slowed down by the vegetation, percolates through the porous limestone hills and emerges from numerous seeps and springs to feed the labyrinth of creeks cut into the limestone over the millennia. Arizona Walnuts, Rough-leaf Dogwoods and American Sycamores spread their leafy branches along the waterways. Delicate Maidenhair and blue-green River Ferns grow along the shaded seeps of ancient grottos, waterfalls, and crystal clear pools, home to many species of fish, spiders, lizards, insects and plants.

The Petersens targeted 350 acres of upland habitat for restoration to benefit the federally endangered Black-capped Vireo and embarked on a program of controlled burning and brush manipulation in order to establish the low vegetation the vireos require for nesting. Bob, a retired Dell Computer Corporation engineer, gave careful consideration to legal and financial implications of attracting additional endangered species to his property. In 2003 he entered into a Safe Harbor Agreement with Environmental Defense and the USFWS. The agreement

includes a baseline survey that specifies the condition and extent of the property representing habitat for the endangered Black-capped Vireo. It ensures Petersen Ranch will not be liable for the loss of any endangered species on the property as long as there is no reduction in the number of species or the amount of habitat that was on the land at the time of the agreement.

The Petersen Ranch has been one of only two private ranches to participate in a research program to determine the effectiveness of con-specific attraction to assist in the establishment of breeding populations of endangered songbirds. The project is funded by the Department of Defense through Fort Hood. Researchers for the University of Illinois have installed call stations with solar-powered stereos that play the Black-capped Vireo calls during the breeding season to simulate established territories and to attract migrating birds.

Bob Petersen has served for two years as Chairman of the Images for Conservation Fund (ICF) Hill Country Advisory Board responsible for the 2006 Pro-Tour of Nature Photography. He is in the process of organizing a Texas Hill Country ICF subsidiary. Emphasizing the educational and economic importance of ecotourism, Petersen Ranch has built dedicated wildlife photography areas situated near water and feed sources and designed to position the photographer with the correct ambient lighting.

Fitzgerald | Little Bluestem beneath Scattered Oaks

Petersen Ranch
Blanco, Texas 78606
Phone: 830-833-0958
www.thepetersenranch.com

Fitzgerald | Sunset over Oak Savannah

Sean Fitzgerald

For someone who got his first camera after college graduation, Sean has come a long way indeed in establishing himself as a top-notch shooter. The former practicing attorney admits to being a "late bloomer" in the field of professional photography. It took a vacation to Europe to first fire his interest in taking pictures. Nature as a subject grew from later travels to various back country destinations in Texas and Colorado. What Sean discovered on these journeys were the many things that were, "just too beautiful not to shoot." He admits, "The more I photographed, the better I wanted to be, and the better I got, the more photographs I wanted to take." It was quite a "vicious loop" but one that has paid dividends in the many award-winning images that, today, bear his copyright.

Aside from Sean's photos gracing the pages of publications such as *Texas Highways*, the *New York Times* and *Outdoor Photographer,* his work also garners attention within various art galleries and museums. This is perhaps appropriate because as Sean states, "Some approach nature photography as being purely documentary. I try to approach it as art. If I can capture the essence of an animal or setting as an abstract painter or sculptor might, I'm usually much happier."

Dallas, Texas
www.seanfitzgerald.com

Fitzgerald | Texas Spiny Lizard

Fitzgerald | Female Black-chinned Hummingbird

Fitzgerald | Treefrog

Fitzgerald | White-eyed Vireo

Fitzgerald | Rock Squirrel

127

Fitzgerald | Little Bluestem

Fitzgerald | Grammia Tiger Moth

Fitzgerald | Spring-fed Grotto

Fitzgerald | Killdeer

About Red Corral Ranch...

Francis | Texas Bluebonnets

Deeply engrained farming and ranching roots guide Colleen and Dr. James Reeves, in their innovative and farsighted stewardship of the 1,100-acre Red Corral Ranch, located in Hays County near Wimberley, Texas. The Reeves purchased the property in 1969 and for years enjoyed the 1934 Limestone House as a weekend and family vacation retreat with their three sons. Inspired by the concept of Holistic Resource Management—that all systems are part of a whole and all wholes are part of an even larger system—the Reeves began to focus their energies on protecting and nurturing the land and wildlife habitats while developing financially viable alternatives for their property.

In 1993, Red Corral Ranch was chosen as the working research site for PlanIt Texas, a coalition formed to resolve conflict between landowners and environmental agencies and to demonstrate that it is possible to have an economically successful ranching operation compatible with the Endangered Species Act. In particular, the listing of the Golden-cheeked Warbler had generated massive conflict in Texas. Ever resistant to outside interference, landowners worried that land values would decline if the warblers were found on their property, making them vulnerable to government regulation. At the same time, the U.S. Fish and Wildlife Service identified the importance of preserving the habitat of mature growth Ashe Juniper and oak groves required for the small black and gold songbirds' spring nesting. Red Corral Ranch, in collaboration with more than twenty PlanIt Texas agencies, dedicated time to test the theory that land can be profitable and managed holistically. The resulting land management legislation and related manual are still in effect.

The Reeves' stated purpose has been to create and sustain "A place to nurture people and the land." To that end, Red Corral Ranch has diversified its production options, increased income from deer hunting and obtained organic certification from the Texas Department of Agriculture. The ranch plans grazing, water and fence changes around the Golden-cheeked Warbler and is working to offer improved habitat for the endangered Black-capped Vireo. Red Corral Ranch also works with the Wildflower Research Center to study how grazing affects wildflowers. The ranch

participates in annual monitoring censuses to determine appropriate White-tailed Deer harvesting. Additionally, records are kept of grass and wildflower abundance, as well as resident and migrating songbird populations.

Red Corral Ranch now includes a bed & breakfast and event facilities designed to offer peace and quiet while providing a sacred space for guests to enhance their own life rhythms as they connect to the land. Visitors enjoy mapped hike and bike trails and a landscaped area of native plants that attracts birds and butterflies for people to enjoy, photograph and study. Shaded beneath towering oaks near the Lodge, a walking labyrinth is lovingly carved into a circular deck. This labyrinth, an exact replica of the one at Chartres Cathedral, provides a quiet place for "prayer, meditation, introspection, quieting the mind and opening the heart."

Visionary leaders, Colleen and James Reeves celebrate the interconnectedness and interdependence of life on this planet in that each individual "whole" is part of the larger whole. They strongly believe that people who own land can no longer function successfully in isolation. "If we spoil our part, the entire whole is affected."

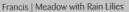

Francis | Meadow with Rain Lilies

Red Corral Ranch
"Nurturing People and the Land"
Colleen and Dr. James Reeves
505 Red Corral Ranch Road
Wimberley, Texas 78676
Phone: 830-833-0206
Reservations: 866-833-4801
www.redcorralranch.com

Photo courtesy of Sherwood Inkley

Michael Francis

A seasonal job at Yellowstone National Park 30 years ago was all it took to get Michael hooked on wildlife photography. The awe-inspiring animals the young employee encountered within the park led to his purchase of a 35mm camera and the creation of his first images of nature. Today, the gifted photographer's works illustrate more than 25 books and grace the pages of such prestigious publications as *Field & Stream, Outdoor Life, Audubon, Time* and *National Wildlife.* The working professional is an active member of the North American Nature Photography Association and served as its president in 2003.

Due to his tenure at Yellowstone, Michael prefers to photograph the continent's larger species. Although he is extremely competent with any outdoor assignment, he readily admits a bias toward "North American big game, including all species of deer, bears and canids."

Michael confesses, he never knows when a special shot will happen but he contends a good photographer can up the odds by knowing the subject matter and placing oneself, "in the right place at the right time." He firmly believes, "It isn't just luck. You make your own just by being out in the field."

Billings, Montana
www.agpix.com/michaelfrancis

Francis | Turkey Vulture

Francis | Giant Redheaded Centipede

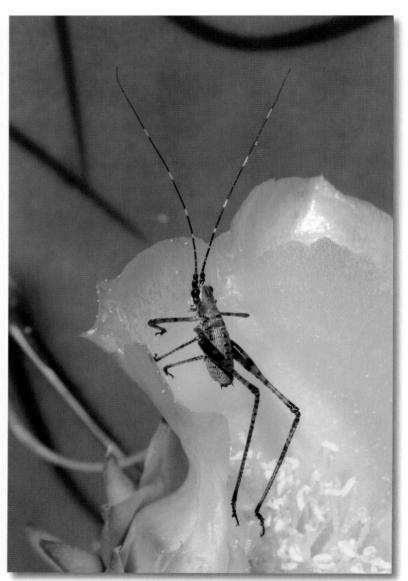

Francis | Immature Scudder's Bush Katydid

Francis | Sunburst Diving Beetle

Francis | Female Northern Cardinal

Francis | Grass Skipper

Francis | Little Bluestem, Live Oak Savannah in the Mist

Francis | Male Wild Turkeys

Francis | Bee Assassin on Lace Cactus

About Rosetta Ranch...

Hendrickson | Live Oak with Prickly Pear and Seep Muhly

Stewardship for their 541-acre Rosetta Ranch fills Kathleen and Robert Earl Keen with the excitement of transformation and discovery. Located in Bandera County near Medina, Texas and acquired by the Keens in 1997, the property was formerly a horse ranch that had been leased for cattle grazing. Conversion to a wildlife valuation and appropriate management strategies have produced marked improvements and a gradual return to the natural beauty of native habitat.

Born in Houston, Robert Earl Keen became a well-known Texas song writer and entertainer. He lived in Austin and Nashville before establishing a home for his family in the heart of the Texas Hill Country. The Keens lived on Rosetta Ranch with their two young daughters until their recent move to nearby Kerrville. A rambling ranch house, horse barns and corrals are located in a picturesque savannah shaded by tall Live Oaks where Hick's Creek and Lost River come together in a natural draw. The Agarita, Yucca, Sotol and Dwarf Palmetto-strewn land rises high above to a craggy dome, offering sweeping views of the homestead below and the green valleys and hazy mountains of the surrounding countryside. There, among the windswept rocks and Prickly Pear Cactus, Robert takes time to survey the world around him. The charred stones of a fire pit testify to campfires and cookouts on the top of the dramatic overlook—a place from which Comanches and Apaches must have once signaled their brethren. Several years before purchasing the property, Robert foresightedly captured the spirit of that breathtaking view in the introductory words he wrote for *Gringo Honeymoon:*

> We were standin' on a mountaintop
> Where the cactus flowers grow
> I was wishen' that the world would stop
> When you said we'd better go.

On a gentler ridge below, Robert built his Scriptorium, the metal-roofed, two-roomed limestone retreat where he spends weeks at a time seeking the mood and inspiration that underscores his music or simply shaking off the

stress from demanding road tours with the REK band. Relaxing in the rough-hewn cedar doorway he can watch the graceful dance of soaring falcons, hawks or turkey buzzards as they ride thermal drafts to swoop and glide, searching the terrain below for unsuspecting prey. At night, brilliant stars dazzle the eyes, while the cooling Hill Country winds carry nocturnal sounds—the twitter of a bird or the plaintive howl of a Coyote.

Dozens of species of butterflies may be found on Rosetta Ranch and Robert tells a story of amazement and delight when he, Kathleen and their eldest daughter unexpectedly rode their horses into a hilltop clearing filled with the hum of millions of gold and black wings fluttering in the morning light. Like migratory birds, Monarch butterflies journey thousands of miles each year along flyways that funnel through Texas from the northern United States and Canada into the jungles of Central Mexico and back again. In fall and again in the springtime, masses of Monarchs may be found among oak groves and hovering over hilltops as they rest and feed on the milkweed that gives them poisonous protection from predator birds and sustains them during their journey.

The Keens wish to continue to preserve the habitat for the creatures whose presence creates "the rhythm for the most extraordinary and beautiful music on earth." The ancient Rosetta Stone, a bridge between archaic and modern language, has become a life paradigm for the Keen family. Rosetta Management, Robert's music management company and record label creates a bridge between the artist and the public. Beautiful Rosetta Ranch exists as an intermediary between the artist, his family and the natural world that is so much a part of the earthy, contemporary cowboy persona he immortalizes in his quirky narrative songs.

Hendrickson | Live Oak Motte

Kathleen and Robert Earl Keen
P.O. Box 400
Medina, Texas 78055
www.robertearlkeen.com

Hendrickson | Scattered Live Oaks,
Live Oak-Juniper Woodland

John Hendrickson

Always a lover of the outdoors, John started photographing raptors at age 17. Those early efforts garnered the attention of others who encouraged the young naturalist to keep shooting. And keep shooting he did, selling his first images while in college. By age 25 his work was published on the prestigious pages of *National Geographic* magazine. Today, the degreed field biologist and environmental educator's award-winning photography continues to be exhibited in major American museums and is featured on the covers and pages of some of the nation's most respected magazines.

Honing his skills over the years and noted by his peers as technically adept, John is particularly lauded for the time he is willing to devote to achieve a superior result. With incredible patience and commitment, the artist freely admits he may "spend days working on a single photograph. But for a great shot, it's worth it."

When asked what he is trying to accomplish through his work, John responds, "I try to create something wonderful to experience but, most importantly, I hope my photographs will remind us of the living beauty that's all around. Perhaps then we will be motivated to preserve our environment."

Clipper Mills, California

Hendrickson | Northern Raccoon

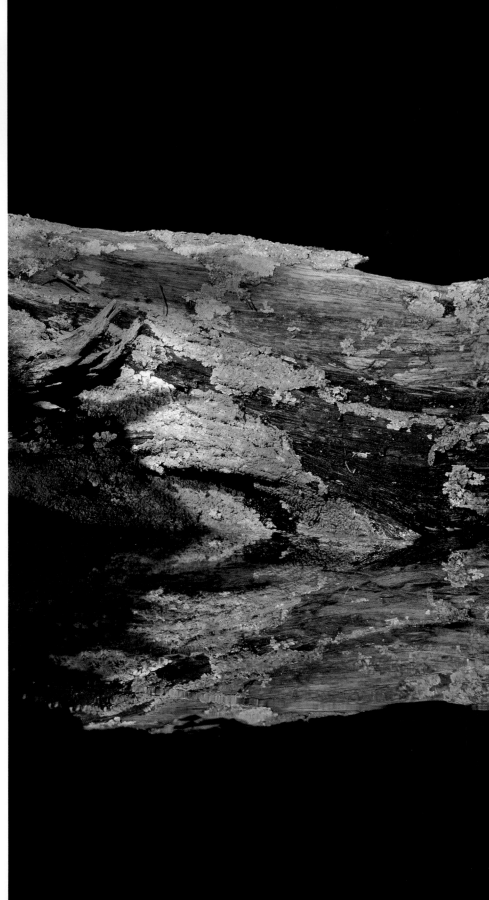

Hendrickson | Belted Kingfisher

Hendrickson | Ironclad Beetle

Hendrickson | Scrub Jay

Hendrickson | Green-backed Heron

Hendrickson | Gray Hairstreak on Cedar Sage

Hendrickson| California Sister on Dakota Vervain

Hendrickson | White-tailed Deer

Hendrickson | Implicit Arches Moth amidst mixed Lichens

About Selah, Bamberger Ranch Preserve...

Woodhouse | Fragrant Mimosa

Inspired by Louis Broomfield's *Pleasant Valley*, the restoration story of worn-out abandoned farms in his native Ohio, entrepreneur J. David Bamberger set out in 1969 to purchase the worst piece of property he could find in Blanco County—over-grazed, juniper-choked acreage which was devoid of water. Massive Ashe Juniper clearing, grass seeding and tree planting, complete with protective cages, have returned the 5,500 acre ranch to a state of natural abundance. Countless springs seep from the hills, supporting a healthy ecosystem that is able to sustain a diverse array of plants and animals.

Once described as the largest habitat restoration project on private land in Texas, the Bamberger Ranch Perserve is an operating ranch that also serves as a natural research laboratory. In the early 1980's Mr. Bamberger, the co-founder and chief executive for Church's Chicken, developed an ingenious plan for the AAZPA (now the American Zoo and Aquarium Association) to set aside a square mile—640 acres—in order to establish a zoo-ranch cooperative designed to develop an oryx population large enough and genetically diverse enough to preserve the Sub-Saharan Scimitar-horned Oryx. Today the handsome white oryx with their reddish-brown markings and long curving horns thrive in their Texas home, free-roaming and capable of survival in the wild. The internationally recognized program at Bamberger Ranch Preserve serves as a model for species preservation.

Ever fascinated by all creatures great and small, Bamberger turned his attention to the Mexican Free-tailed Bat. After years of volunteering with Bat Conservation International's Bracken Cave project, plans were made to build a man-made bat cave on the ranch, large enough to house a million bats. Since its completion in 1998 the "chiroptorium" seasonally houses tens of thousands of bats and supplies the ranch with guano.

The ranch's most recent project for conservation and species survival involves the endangered Texas Snowbell (*Styrax texana*), a small understory tree that inhabits the limestone cliffs of the western edge of the Hill Country, producing a bell-shaped white flower in mid-April. J. David Bamberger's quest to find seeds and to propagate and develop genetic material for recovery and reintroduction has grown into a federally recognized program relying upon the unprecedented cooperation of landowners. In 2003, a recovery plan goaled to reintroduce 500 trees on public and private lands in their native habitat.

Because education and "people ranching" are priorities, J. David and Margaret Bamberger share the ranch and their experience in habitat restoration through workshops, seminars and field trips. The master promoter and motivator has turned his focus to marketing conservation. Accordingly, Bamberger Ranch Preserve offers educational workshops and models for all seven Wildlife Management Use Requirements for Agricultural Tax Appraisal. Selah is accredited with the Texas Education Agency to provide appropriate environmental education to schoolchildren. The preserve is maintained and operated by a dedicated staff and loyal volunteers.

For all of his endeavors, Bamberger applies a key maxim: "It's easier to initiate an action than to sustain it–you've got to think of the economic ability to carry the plan through." As they look to the future, the Bambergers have placed the property for perpetuity in a foundation, The Bamberger Ranch Preserve, which assures the land continues as a living lab and learning center. To J. David, "Selah (a Biblical term from the Book of Psalms, inviting one to stop, pause and reflect) is like Walden was to Thoreau." The legacy is one of coalition building; the spirit of exploration; practical business application; love and respect for the preservation of nature's bounty.

Woodhouse | Limestone Bluff

Selah, Bamberger Ranch Preserve
2341 Blue Ridge Dr.
Johnson City, Texas 78636
Phone: 830-868-2630
www.bambergerranch.org

Woodhouse | Sunset over Selah

Jeremy Woodhouse

"Citizen of the world" comes to mind when one hears the name Jeremy Woodhouse. His birth in Nigeria, rearing in Pakistan and Argentina, followed by a stint as a graphic designer in South Africa and the United Kingdom before his incarnation into a full-time professional photographer based in the United States, give this unique individual an international perspective few can match. Today, the wanderlust continues as he and his camera pursue assignments in scores of countries across the globe.

Known for his panoramic images of urban skylines, the adaptable shooter is equally at ease in the bush. It was in South Africa that Jeremy originally developed his passion for wildlife and environmental photography. When he's not shooting some exotic cityscape, the intrepid traveler might be photographing a herd of gregarious elephants at a Botswanan water hole, snapping timid jackrabbits in arid South Texas or capturing dramatic panoramas of Australia's Ayer's Rock. His work, consistently praised for its artistic composition, has earned recognition internationally through venues such as the BBC/British Gas Wildlife Photographer of the Year competition and photography exhibitions at the Smithsonian Institute in Washington D.C. and London's Natural History Museum.

When quizzed on what's needed for successful shooting in the wild, a smiling

Jeremy responds, "Planning, knowledge of the quarry, quick reactions and a *whole lot of luck.*"

McKinney, Texas
www.pixelchrome.com

Woodhouse | Live Oak

Woodhouse | Gray Fox

Woodhouse | Eastern Screech Owl

Woodhouse | Western Ribbon Snake

Woodhouse | Great Blue Heron

Woodhouse | Mourning Dove

Woodhouse | Immature Green Fool Grasshopper

Woodhouse | Spider (species unknown)

About Stowers Ranch Company...

Kaehler | Great Blue Heron

George Arthur Stowers, the founder of Stowers Furniture Company headquartered in San Antonio, established Stowers Ranch in 1904 as a cattle ranch, game management area and hunting preserve. In 1922, the family built a ranch house of native stone with a sweeping double staircase in the gracious style of Teddy Roosevelt era hunting lodges. The property is now owned by his grandson and great-grandchildren and offers hunting for White-tailed and exotic bucks and wild turkey, along with bird watching, game viewing, nature photography and hiking. The 11,250-acre ranch is located at the headwaters of the North Fork of the Guadalupe River, approximately 13 miles west of Hunt, Texas, in Kerr County.

A hunting enthusiast and preservationist, Mr. Stowers introduced Elk from Colorado in the early 1900's and high-fenced the ranch for the purpose of managing the Elk and White-tailed Deer. Later the Elk were replaced by freely roaming herds of Axis Deer, Fallow Deer, Sika, Aoudad and Black Buck Antelope, all of which are found on the ranch today. Stirrup-high grasses and open savannahs, oak and hardwood forests and breathtaking vistas are reminiscent of the Texas Hill Country encountered by settlers in the early nineteenth century.

Stowers Ranch's management practices have created a healthy watershed producing plentiful seeps and springs to feed Flat Rock Creek and the North Fork of the Guadalupe River. These meandering streams contain several species of panfish, catfish and Smallmouth Bass and furnish habitat to Great Blue Herons and itinerant ducks. A dramatic limestone cliff regally stands watch over placid Bonnibel Lake, providing sheltering crevices and ledges as roosts for American Bald Eagles and Golden Eagles. Along the shore below, Rio Grande Turkeys seek shelter in the tall sycamore and elm trees near the life-giving water. On a spring day, dozens of ink black Ravens swoop and glide with a woosh of wings in an age-old mating ritual. The Stowers Ranch cave, a complex array of large rooms and parallel passages that is the tenth longest cave in Texas, is home for a colony of Mexican Free-tailed Bats.

Inspired by Allan Savory's philosophy for holistic management of natural resources, the family has coordinated with Texas Parks & Wildlife Department, the nearby Kerr Wildlife Management Area and federal support programs

over the past 35 years to nurture and protect water, land and wildlife. Placing an emphasis on brush clearing, Stowers Ranch works actively with the National Resource Conservation Service to control Ashe Juniper re-growth by hand cutting and use of chainsaws and hydraulic shears. Controlled burns of approximately 20% of the ranch each year encourage emergence of a wide variety of native grasses and forbs. The ranch maintains cattle in a single herd, and imposes tight "time controlled" grazing. To promote native plant growth and diversity of plant species, wildlife is carefully monitored and numbers are reduced as needed through hunting, capture and sale.

These enlightened landowners feel a strong sense of responsibility to prevent land fragmentation and to protect watersheds and wildlife, while providing access for visitors to experience the natural bounty of the beautiful Texas Hill Country. In addition to the cattle operation, the ranch hosts carefully guided three-day hunts and offers accommodations for up to 18 people in air-conditioned, rustic log cabins and a frame ranch house.

The family views eco-tourism as an important twenty-first century initiative—for the ranch, as well as for public education and recreation. The ranch participates in spring breeding bird surveys and Audubon Christmas bird counts that have identified over 50 different species. Stowers Ranch has entered into a Safe Harbor Agreement with Environmental Defense, actively protecting endangered Golden-cheeked Warblers and creating a 40-acre sanctuary for endangered Black-capped Vireos. Game viewing, bird watching, wildlife photography and hiking are available by reservation. For the photography enthusiast, Stowers Ranch Company offers specialized photo blinds with water sources and feeders along with workshops and retreats.

Kaehler | Oak Woodland

Stowers Ranch Company
Richard and Josephine Smith
625 Stowers Ranch Road
Hunt, Texas 78024
Phones: 830-238-4345, 830-238-4346
stowersrch@aol.com
www.stowersranch.com

Kaehler | Sotol Tips, Ashe Juniper, Grass Savannah

Wolfgang Kaehler

"Doing what it takes" is a primary reason why Wolfgang enjoys an international reputation as a premier wildlife photographer. An example would have to include his eye-level shot of two Galapagos iguanas backed by a distant volcano. To achieve the desired composition, the German-born photographer was required to crawl painfully across many feet of barnacle-encrusted rock. The short-term result was multiple (and serious) lacerations across his arms, legs and torso. The long-term is a photograph that continues to enjoy repeated publication.

As a past expedition cruise ship photographer, Wolfgang had the opportunity to explore and photograph some of the planet's most remote regions. His Antarctic image collection is one of the largest and most significant in the world. From that collection, Wolfgang was awarded first prize in the Compositions and Form category of the BBC Wildlife Photographer of the Year competition for his "Penguins on the Ice" photo—chosen from 8,500 other entries. Currently, Wolfgang travels extensively on assignments from various publications, travel companies and advertising agencies.

When asked what is essential to a successful image, Wolfgang offers, "The elements of great nature photography can vary but the best should all possess a unique composition—which is not always easy because you can't control an animal's movements."

Bellevue, Washington
www.kaehlerphoto.com

Kaehler | Northern Raccoon

156

Kaehler | Hog-nosed Skunk

Kaehler | Red-eared Slider

Kaehler | Green Anole

Kaehler | Killdeer

Kaehler | Western Diamondback Rattlesnake

Kaehler | Funnel Spider

Kaehler | Virginia Creeper

Kaehler | Rain Lily

2006 Pro-Tour Sponsors

The success of the inaugural Images for Conservation Fund (ICF) Pro-Tour of Nature Photography was determined by a group of individuals, communities, businesses and corporations who provided the funding that allowed the operations staff and volunteers to create the first and richest professional nature photographic tournament ever held. The Images for Conservation Fund is grateful for their support. They have helped to make the ICF Pro-Tour concept into a powerful reality.

Sponsoring the ICF Pro-Tour demonstrates a visible commitment to our world, our children and our society. Our human destiny is truly intertwined with nature–from the food we eat to the serene and exhilarating experiences that can be found only in nature.

Community Sponsors

ICF Hometown of Nature Photography in the Texas Hill Country

Bandera Convention & Visitors Bureau
Fredericksburg Convention & Visitors Bureau
Gillespie County Economic Development Board

AEP Texas, an electricity delivery company serving south and west Texas, is proud to be an original sponsor of the Images for Conservation Fund Pro-Tour of Nature Photography.

A unit of American Electric Power

Business & Foundation Sponsors

AEP Texas
CEMEX
Toyota
The Loring Cook Foundation
Texas Farm & Ranch Magazine
Munoz Investment Banking Group
City of Kerrville Convention & Visitors Bureau
Ellis Koeneke Ramirez, LLP
Fredericksburg Convention & Visitors Bureau
Gillespie County Economic Development Board
H-E-B
The Brown Foundation, Inc.
Alamo Forest Products
Alamo Lumber Company

Denver Digital Imaging Center, A Division of the Slideprinter
    Official Photofinishing Lab of the ICF Pro-Tour
TMI, the Episcopal School of Texas
Gallagher Headquarters
Nature Photographers Network
Bandera, Texas - Cowboy Capital of the World
Arthur Morris / BIRDS AS ART
The Stai Family Foundation
Inn of the Hills (Kerrville)
Stowers Ranch Company
Rudy & Myla Schmuck Memorial Fund
Alfred S. Gage Family Foundation
Frost Bank
Bank of America

Individual Sponsors

John & Audrey Martin
    in honor of their parents and Georgia Mason
Linda Price May in Memory of David May
Howard & Millicent Mason
Rachel Blancas
Pat Rangel
George & Claire Vaughan

Roger A. Zessin
Sherwood & Bebe Inkley
Georgia Mason
Jose A. Lopez, M.D.
Bob & Cindy Petersen
Tony Sauer

Book Patrons

H-E-B
South Texas Money Management LLC
CEMEX
AEP Texas

Bank of America - Private Bank
A.G. Edwards & Sons - Roger Zessin
Arthur & Jennifer Cahoon
Copperfield & Katy Prairie Allergy

The ICF Launch Committee
Alamo Heights - Terrell Hills
    Garden Club, GCA
Annandale Ranch
Applied Digital Science
    Topp Robertson
Katharine Armstrong
Bamberger Ranch Preserve
Tom Barrett Optical Inc.
Joe Donnelly Carpentry
Mike & Sandra Dorris
Jon & Dana Fletcher
Millicent Bleakney & Howard Mason
A.G. Edwards & Sons
    Bill Martin   Greg Douglas
    Jerry Raders   Teresa Hunter
Ellis, Koeneke, & Ramirez, LLP
Environmental Defense

Mrs. Kittie Nelson Ferguson
Mrs. Kittie West Hughes
Flying A Ranch
Dale R. Franz
Fredericksburg Convention &
    Vistors Bureau
Kevin Graham
Hayden & Cunningham, PLC
Bob & Cassie Hixon - Estrella Ranch
Sherwood & Bebe Inkley
Robert Earl & Kathleen Keen
    Keen Productions
Kerrville Convention & Visitors Bureau
Chuck & Sharon Knibbe - Knibbe Ranch
John Kothmann - Red Creek Nature Ranch
Gary & Gwen Krause - Krause Ranch
David & Myrna Langford
Sharron & Larry Jay

George & Toni Martin
Milby Moore
Jose A. Lopez, MD
Lower Colorado River Authority
Marriott, Curt Pfannstiel
John & Audrey Martin
Anne O. Meyer
Dr. Scott Miller
Palmer Moe
Dr. Dolores Corona Mora
Michael A. Murphy
Natural Bridge Caverns
Naturally Curious, Inc.
Nature Conservancy
Rolf & Karen Nussbaumer
Peaceful Springs Nature Preserve
    David & Cynthia Castleberry
Al Perry

Bob & Cindy Petersen
Plateau Land & Wildlife Management
Maria & Erik Pronske
    Capital Anesthesiology Associates
Carol Rausch
Alice L. Robertson - in memory of my
    dad, George Edward Robertson
Seton Family of Hospitals
Ted & Suzanne Stewart
Stowers Ranch
Technical Focus, Jere May
Karen Elizabeth Shrader, MD
Ken & Patty Taylor
Texas Parks & Wildlife Employees
Jerry & Diane Turner
T Bar 6 Ranch, Blanco, Texas
George & Claire Vaughan
V&S Vaughan & Sons, Inc.

Knibbe Ranch | Franz | Carolina Chickadee

The Images for Conservation Fund Pro-Tour of Nature Photography thanks CEMEX for its continuing support.

Peaceful Springs Nature Preserve | Ulrich | White-tailed Deer

2006 Pro-Tour Partners

The inaugural Pro-Tour event was a resounding success because of the people and organizations that made outstanding commitments and contributions to the event and our mission. Our partners are among those groups: they signed on early giving us credibility, they made commitments and fulfilled them, and they gave us highly qualified people to use where we needed them most. ICF is grateful and indebted to all of the following:

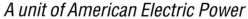

A unit of American Electric Power

ENERGY • WATER • COMMUNITY SERVICES

SAVING THE LAST GREAT PLACES ON EARTH

Go Digital, Go to the Zone!

ENVIRONMENTAL DEFENSE

finding the ways that work

SMITH
FANKHAUSER
VOIGT &
WATSON, PLLC

Plateau
Land & Wildlife Management

cockrell printing company
www.cockrellprinting.com
Ken Gaskins

TEXAS
PUBLIC RADIO

Photography 414
North American Nature Photography Association
Conservation International
The Conservation Fund Wildlife Habitat Council

ICF National Board of Directors

- John F. Martin, Chairman
  Edinburg, Texas
- Connie K. Bransilver, National Vice-Chairman
  Naples, Florida
- Bob Petersen, Texas Vice-Chairman
  Austin, Texas
- Carol Rausch, Secretary
  McAllen, Texas
- Miguel A. Nevárez, PhD, Treasurer
  Edinburg, Texas
- Katharine Armstrong
  Austin, Texas
- Arthur L. Cahoon
  Jacksonville, Florida
- Thomas D. Koeneke
  McAllen, Texas
- Edward H. Muñoz
  Far Hills, New Jersey
- Gabby Salazar, Youth Director
  Pleasant Garden, North Carolina
- Roberto Zambrano
  Monterrey, Mexico
- Roger A. Zessin
  Corpus Christi, Texas

Hill Country Advisory Board

The success of any organization in accomplishing its mission is not in the vision of its founder or the value of the desired outcome, but the quality of the individuals who commit time, work and inspiration to the program.

- Bob Petersen, Chairman
- Katharine Armstrong
- Dayna Boren Cartwright
- David Barr Dunham
- Rod Gardner
- Larry Jones, AEP Texas
  Publicity Chairman
- Karen Kilfeather
  Awards Co-Chairman
- Wallace Klussmann
- David K. Langford
- Stephen Maynard
- Stan Meador
- Shelly Scroggs Plante, Texas Parks & Wildlife Department
  Symposium Chairman & Awards Co-Chairman
- Erik Pronske, MD
  Symposium Assistant Chairman (Landowners)
- Pat Rangel
  Book Production & Editor
- Diane Solether Smith
  Lead Book Writer & Exhibits Chairman
- Claire Vaughan
  Launch Party Chairman

Distinguished Judges...

Rosamund Kidman Cox
Former Editor of *BBC Wildlife Magazine*

Rosamund Kidman Cox, former editor of *BBC Wildlife Magazine*, has worked as a commissioning editor of natural history books and is author of a series of children's nature books. She has been a judge and organizer of the BBC International Wildlife Photographer of the Year competition since 1981.

Stephen B. Freligh
Publisher/Editor-in-Chief, *Nature's Best*

Steve Freligh is the founder and president of the Nature's Best Foundation. The foundation's award-winning publication, *Nature's Best*; the prestigious Nature's Best International Photography Awards ceremony; and ongoing photography exhibits at the Smithsonian National Museum of Natural History in Washington, DC, offer the public extraordinary views of nature.

Art Wolfe
World-renowned Wildlife Photographer

Washington photographer Art Wolfe is one of the most internationally acclaimed and published nature photographers of our time. He is a passionate spokesperson for conservation and serves on the advisory boards of The North American Nature Photography Association, the Nature's Best Foundation and the Wildlife Conservation Society.